1

AROUND 1700: THE HEY-DAY OF THE HAND-WORKER

How goods were made in early eighteenth-century England.

A Workers by hand – the woollen trades
B Stockings, ribbons, scissors and nails – other hand-working trades
C Trading, transport and towns
D Energy, power and technology
E Skills section: the use of sources

Manufacturing around 1700

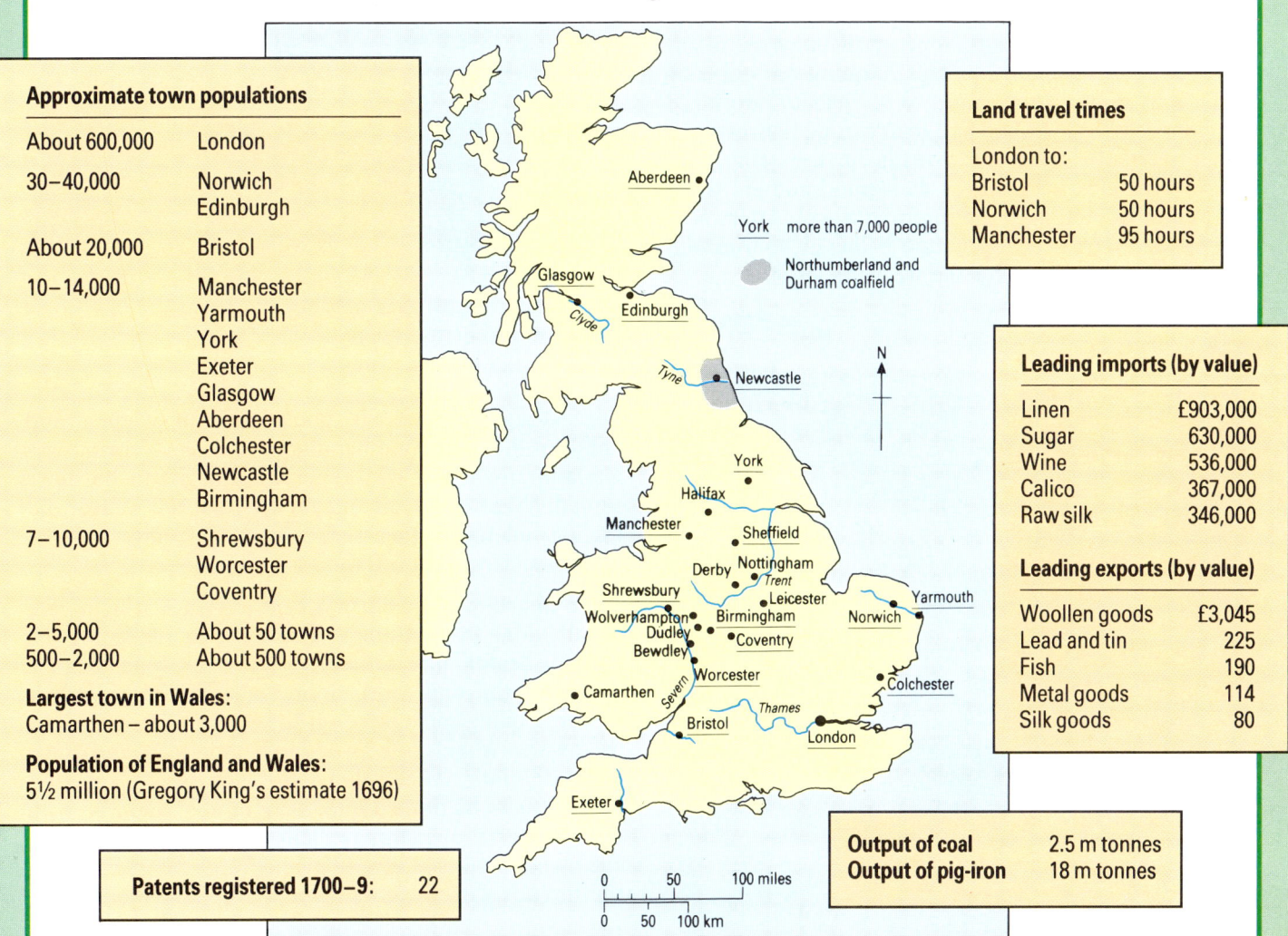

Approximate town populations

About 600,000	London
30–40,000	Norwich
	Edinburgh
About 20,000	Bristol
10–14,000	Manchester
	Yarmouth
	York
	Exeter
	Glasgow
	Aberdeen
	Colchester
	Newcastle
	Birmingham
7–10,000	Shrewsbury
	Worcester
	Coventry
2–5,000	About 50 towns
500–2,000	About 500 towns

Largest town in Wales:
Camarthen – about 3,000

Population of England and Wales:
5½ million (Gregory King's estimate 1696)

Patents registered 1700–9: 22

Land travel times

London to:
Bristol	50 hours
Norwich	50 hours
Manchester	95 hours

Leading imports (by value)

Linen	£903,000
Sugar	630,000
Wine	536,000
Calico	367,000
Raw silk	346,000

Leading exports (by value)

Woollen goods	£3,045
Lead and tin	225
Fish	190
Metal goods	114
Silk goods	80

Output of coal 2.5 m tonnes
Output of pig-iron 18 m tonnes

Before you read on:

a) What communities do you know with populations similar to those of eighteenth-century towns?
b) How would you rate the importance of woollen-cloth making to Britain's overseas trade around 1700?
c) Why do you think the number of patents has been included?
d) What are the present-day travel times from London to Bristol and Manchester?

A WORKERS BY HAND

Around 1700 the word 'industry' meant hard work, the opposite of idleness. The term for making goods was 'manufacture', from the Latin for 'making by hand'. People would not have understood a discussion about whether women should be wage-earners or home-makers. They would have been just as amazed at the idea that children should not take part in wage-earning. It is likely that the greatest number of hours put into manufacturing was done by women and children.

Woollen manufacture

In many parts of Britain, ploughing, harvesting and threshing gave all-the-year work to male farm labourers but the largest item in their homes was the spinning wheel, which was the most common piece of manufacturing equipment in the country. Spinning was only one of the jobs done in the home. Wool had to be picked clean of brambles, washed and then carded between two wire brushes to make the threads lie the same way. These were jobs for children and grandmothers while other adult women used the spinning wheel. Afterwards they handed the yarn back to their helpers who wound it onto reels and bobbins for the weaver's loom.

A

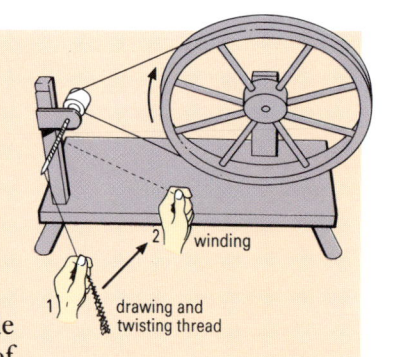

The spinner attaches an end of the fibre to the spindle and draws it out with her left hand while turning the wheel to give a twist to the thread. The thread has to be held at an angle so it can slip off the tip of the spindle. Once it is twisted the spinner changes position to wind the thread.

Traditional spinning, 1814.

1. What is the old woman doing?
2. Try explaining how spinning was done.

B

A handloom weaver.

3. What is the weaver holding in his hand?
4. How did he use his feet?

On average it took six households of women and children to supply one handloom weaver. Weaving was work for men and was generally thought to be more skilled. What that really meant was that the weaver did the job full-time. His assistant was a boy, often his son, who was learning the trade as an apprentice.

After weaving, the cloth went on to stages which were usually done in workshops. 'Fulling' was thickening the cloth by beating it in a trough of water and fuller's earth. This was the only work done with the help of water power. Fulling mills were on the banks of streams and their water-wheels lifted wooden hammers up and down onto the cloth. After fulling, the cloth was taken to a dye-house to be dipped into heated water coloured with dyes made from plants. Finally it went to a shearing shed where it was stretched over a frame for men to trim the threads with huge hand-held cropping shears.

In some parts all these operations might be done in one district. In the south-west cattle were more important than crops so there was little sowing, harvesting and threshing, and labourers could be part-time weavers. Farmers often owned a dye-house or a fulling mill which they might open only in the winter when there was plenty of water and little other work. This combination of farming and woollen manufacture was even more important in the Pennine districts of Yorkshire. Daniel Defoe found the hillsides around Halifax divided into small landholdings. The owners kept a few animals on their land but had turned their home into a workshop.

C

Among the manufacturers' houses are likewise scattered an infinite number of cottages or small dwellings in which dwell the workmen who are employed, the women and children of whom are also busy carding, spinning, &c so that...all can gain their bread, even from the youngest to the ancient; hardly any thing above four years old, but its hands are sufficient.

...if we knocked at the door of any master manufacturer, we presently saw a house full of lusty fellows, some at the dye-fat [*vat*], some dressing the cloths, some in the loom...all hard at work.

D. Defoe, *Tour thro' the whole island of Great Britain*, 1720–7

5. Is there any sign that Defoe disapproves of children's work?

It was more usual for manufacturing to be spread over a large area. For instance, Norfolk was one of the busiest farming counties but it also held Britain's second largest city, Norwich. It was the leading centre for weaving worsted, the cloth made from the longest wool fibres. In the 1720s Daniel Defoe described where their raw material came from:

D

The vast manufactures carried on by the Norwich weavers, employs all the country around in spinning yarn, besides many packs of yarn which they receive from other countries, even from as far as Yorkshire and Westmoreland.

D. Defoe, *Tour thro' the whole island of Great Britain*, 1720–7

6. What difference does Defoe describe between cloth manufacture in Norwich and in Yorkshire?

Masters and workers

The man who ran a widespread organisation like this was the master clothier (or cloth-ier). He was a wealthy merchant who supplied the home-based carders and spinners with raw wool and then saw that the material went from stage to stage until he had bales of finished cloth which he could sell. He paid the workers in each stage by piece rates and it could be many months before he got any money back from sales.

In a modern factory, assembly lines carry goods from one stage to the next. Eighteenth-century workers made weekly visits to the master clothier's agent, or putter-out, to take their finished work, be paid and collect materials for their next stint. Pay disputes were constantly breaking out. Old laws gave the county magistrates, or JPs, the power to fix wage-rates and workers often took complaints to them. If the masters or JPs would not alter the payments there was the possibility of a riot. In 1726 weavers in Somerset complained that the:

E

A description of a master clothier in 1757:

One Person with a great Stock and a large Credit, buys the Wool, pays for the Spinning, Weaving, Milling, Dying, Shearing, Dressing etc etc. That is, he is the Master of the Whole Manufacture from first to last, and perhaps employs a thousand Persons under him. This is the Clothier, whom all the Rest are to look upon as their Paymaster.

Josiah Tucker, *Instructions for travellers*, 1757

7. What does Joseph Tucker mean by 'stock' and 'credit'? Why did each have to be large?

'Difference they have with their masters, the Clothiers ...is, that they have increased their Work, and diminished their Wages.'

A large group of the protesters visited a town where several clothiers lived and

'went into several Houses with a Paper to settle their Wages, and where their Demands were complied with, and smooth words given, they did no harm, but where there was any Hesitation, or what they call uncivil Treatment, the Windows paid for it.'

Farley's Bristol Newspaper, 10 December 1726

Masters, too, had their grouses which often sound like ones we hear today. 'It is not those who are absolutely idle that injure the public so much as they who work but half their time' wrote one man in 1752. What he had in mind was Saint Monday when little work was done.

F

Saint Monday.

8. Which forms of 'recreation' can you see?
9. What evidence is there that these people are workers?

B STOCKINGS, RIBBONS, SCISSORS AND NAILS

Woollen-cloth making was the most important textile manufacture but it was not the only one. The east midlands contained the homes of the framework knitters. This was a trade for the whole family. Children and women carded and span, and handed the thread to the man at the frame. He was often a men's-wear specialist because he was knitting hose or stockings in an age when men showed their legs and women didn't. After hose, the main use for knitting frames was to make shaped pieces which were sown into waistcoats.

Framework knitting was controlled by master hosiers. Most had their warehouses in Derby, Leicester or Nottingham, and knitters could spend up to two days a week travelling from the villages to collect work. Knitters in Leicestershire, which was a sheep-raising county, used mostly wool. In Derbyshire they made finer hose with silk imported from Italy. Nottinghamshire knitters were beginning to use a new fibre – sea-island cotton from the West Indies.

A

1. Knitters are often shown in rooms with other people while weavers are usually drawn alone. Why might this be?

In the early eighteenth century, Lancashire's merchant clothiers were developing good lines in imitations of the most fashionable textiles. The trouble with wool was that it was difficult to change the cut, colour and patterns for the most stylish dress. The person who could afford to be fashionable turned to linen, imported from Ireland where flax was grown, or to calico, which was a cotton cloth from Calicut in India.

The Lancashire merchants found they could cash in on the fashion with fustian woven from a mixture of linen for the warp (up-down threads) and sea-island cotton for the weft. It could be block-printed with methods copied from India and was hard to tell from the finest calico.

B

This is how Samuel Crompton remembered his infancy in the 1740s:

> Soon after I was able to walk I was employed in the cotton manufacture. My mother used to bat the cotton wool on a wire riddle. It was then put into a deep brown mug with a strong ley of soap suds. My mother then tucked up my petticoats about my waist and put me in the tub to tread on the cotton at the bottom. When the mug was quite full, the soap suds were poured off, and each separate dollop of wool...were then placed on the bread rack under the beams of the kitchen-loft to dry. My mother and grandmother carded the cotton wool by hand...When carded they were put aside ...ready for spinning.

Quoted in G French, *Life of Samuel Crompton*, 1860

2. List the manufacturing operations done in this household.

Women's dresses were often decorated with silk ribbons, made on narrow looms in and around Coventry. In Coventry itself a family home might have several looms with the man, his wife and older children all working on them. In the villages, men were often coal-miners and here ribbon weaving was a woman's trade. She was more likely to be making the cheaper plain black ribbons – and be earning less for just as much work. Like cloth and hosiery, ribbon manufacturing had its masters who imported the silk from Italy.

Outside the main branches of textiles there were other examples of cottage work for women and children. In many parts of the country they worked as lace-makers, but there was also making gloves, plaiting straw for hats or making baskets out of willow. Like the cloth, stockings and ribbons, these goods were made with materials supplied by merchants and could end up being sold in London or another large town and even in Europe or America.

The iron trades

You found iron-workers where there was wood on the surface and iron ore in the ground. Miners dug out the ore while charcoal burners cut the wood into heaps of faggots and slowly charred them. What happened next was described by a visitor to the furnace owned by the Birmingham iron-master, Sampson Lloyd:

C

> Next day we went to see an Iron Furnace at a small distance from Birmingham, where the iron ore is smelted and run into pigs... The iron stone or ore being mixed with a quantity of charcoal, is put in at the top... as it descends the fire burns more fiercely being blown by two pairs of monstrous bellows, which moving alternately by means of a water-wheel, throw in a continued stream of air ...When a sufficient quantity is thus fluxed, the metal is let out into a wide frame in the ground, filled with sand which is hollow'd into... the shape of the pigs of iron and many pigs are cast together joining to a long middle-piece call'd the sow.
>
> *Four Topographical Letters written in July 1755 from a Gentleman of London to his Brother and Sister in Town,* 1757

3. How did 'pig-iron' get its name?
4. What did the writer mean by 'fluxed'?
5. Why was a building where this was done known as a blast furnace?

Pig-iron was only a basic raw material. The smelting had passed so much carbon into it that it was too brittle for use. So it first had to be taken to a forge. Here it was reheated in an open fire until it was soft enough to beat. It was then worked on by men with hammers or sometimes by a helve hammer lifted up and down by a water-wheel. The heating and the beating took most of the carbon out and it was now not a pig but a bar of wrought [*worked*] iron.

Bars were too large to be turned into the iron products of the early 1700s so they had to be cut down. Sampson Lloyd's vistors saw this in a slitting mill he owned:

D

> They take a large iron bar, and with a huge pair of shears, worked by a water-wheel, cut it into lengths of about a foot each; these pieces are put into a furnace, and heated red-hot, then taken out and put between a couple of steel rollers, which draw them to the length of about four feet, and the breadth of about three inches... they are immediately put between two other rollers which, having a number of sharp edges fitting each other like scissors, cut the bar as it passes through, into about eight square rods; after the rods are cold they are tied up in bundles for the nailer's use.
>
> *Four Topographical Letters,* 1757

6. Which operations described in the letter can you see in the picture?

An iron-master like Sampson Lloyd usually owned blast furnaces, forges and slitting mills yet they were not close together. Each needed a good supply of water so the master had to build them a mile or so apart even on the same stream. Once his forges and mills had produced the bar or rods, the iron-master sold them to iron-mongers.

The iron-monger was the equivalent of the master clothier. He employed hundreds of workers making iron goods by hand in their own homes. In south Staffordshire you could see men on the roads weighed down with bundles of iron rods they had collected from iron-mongers in Birmingham or Dudley. They were taking them to the tiny workshops built onto the side of their cottages. Here they would hammer and file while women and children worked the hand bellows, fed the fire or turned the grinding wheel.

Each village or group of villages had a specialism. It might be farming tools such as scythes, or locks, or chains, or fancier goods such as shoe buckles. As in textiles, the work was often broken down into different stages. Different parts of locks were made in different places and there were three separate districts for buckle-making. The frame was made in one, the hook in another while workers in the third assembled the two together. The largest group of all were the nailers. This was the least skilled and the poorest paid iron trade and it took whole families long hours of toil to earn a bare living. Nailers hardly ever owned land but the more skilled workers often combined iron manufacture with work on their own farms.

The other main iron-working area was in Sheffield and the villages around. The hills provided good quality grinding stones and the handworkers of the district had come to specialise in tools which required sharp edges such as knives, scissors and files.

C TRADING, TRANSPORT AND TOWNS

In 1700 there was nothing like the mass market we are part of when we shop at stores which sell clothes or furniture. The families who made the cloth, stockings, knives and nails in their cottages had little spending power. Many still made their own clothes and the few items of furniture in their bare homes. They made rush-lights by dipping rushes in the bacon fat left in the pan. If they needed an earthenware jug, a cooking pot or a bit of lace or ribbon it could be bought from a travelling pedlar or by a walk into the town on market day.

The traders

The master clothiers, hosiers, and iron-mongers had three important outlets for the goods their handworkers made. One was the government which bought in bulk for the army and navy. It gave orders for stockings for soldiers in lots of 10,000. Then there was exporting. A good half of all the cloth was sent overseas, mostly to Europe but some to colonies in the West Indies and America. Some iron goods went to Africa to be sold in exchange for slaves who were shipped to the colonies. Others such as hoes, knives, horse-hoes and buckles went direct to the colonies. The third important point of sale was in the larger towns. Shops were changing from being a room with a counter open to the street where a craftsman sold his own goods. They were becoming bow-fronted places with inside counters where the keeper sold goods he had bought from merchants.

Iron-mongers and master clothiers employed salesmen, known as riders, who sold goods direct to pedlars and shopkeepers. They could also sell in bulk to a merchant or trader who might have his own riders or might be in the export business. Such deals were sometimes made at the annual fairs that were still held at a few places. But woollen goods were so bulky that it was easier to send samples to cloth halls where traders could inspect them and place orders. Cloth halls and blanket halls were built in many towns in the early eighteenth century.

A

A job advertisement.

A sober and steady man of unexceptionable character, brought up to or well understands the wholesale manufacturing trade of Birmingham and Wolverhampton in the iron and toy business, and if acquainted with Sheffield business it would be the more agreeable. Must be well qualified to ride journeys in the above branches for taking orders, settling accounts when on journeys, and at home to be employed in the warehouse business... Any person that can answer the above description is desired to send a letter in his own hand.

Aris's Birmingham Gazette, 7 January 1759

1. What would be the usual term for the man who placed this advertisement?
2. What did he mean by the 'Sheffield business'?
3. What were the rider's duties?

Transport

Once the sale was agreed, the merchants had to move the goods. Many started their journey on packhorses moving nose-to-tail across the hills and over hump-backed bridges. Progress slowed when the loads reached the clay lowlands. A team of horses could pull a waggon through the dried ruts in summer but the winter mud made many routes impossible. Waterways were easier. Some goods could make the whole journey by river but others went part of the way on coastal ships. There were ports on the rivers as well as the seacoast. One of the great arteries was the River Severn. Goods from as far away as Lancashire were loaded on to boats at Shrewsbury and further down there were Bewdley and Stourbridge which specialised in iron goods from the midlands. When they reached Bristol some were transferred to ships sailing overseas and the rest went onto coastal vessels sailing to ports around the coast.

B

Worcester, a port on the river Severn. The boats are trows used for carrying goods on the river.

4. Use page 1 to say where Worcester ranked in population size in the early eighteenth century.
5. What were the two ways of moving the trows?

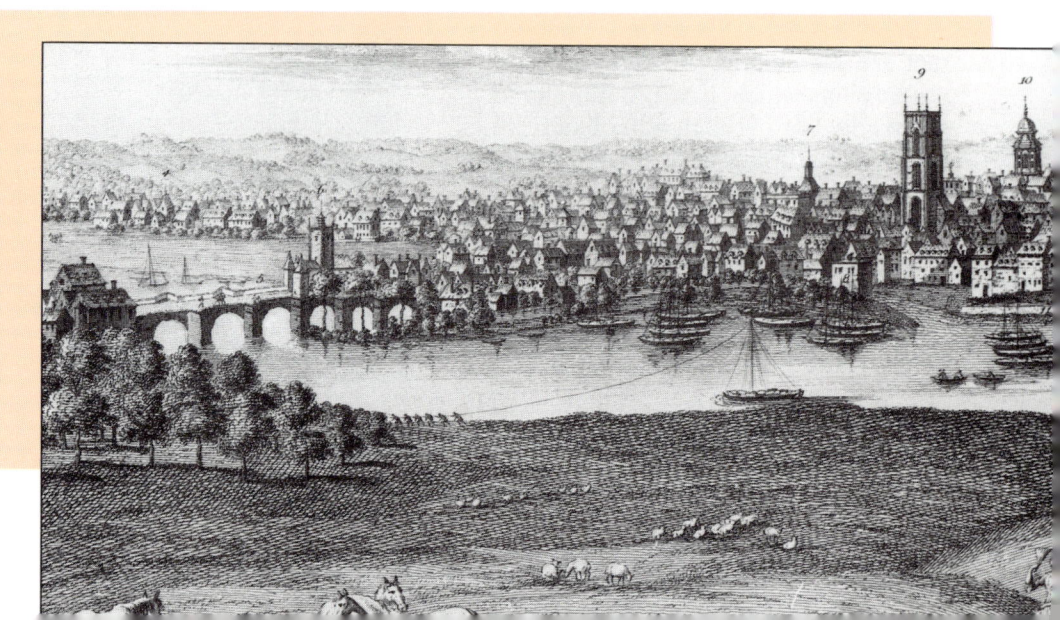

Market towns

Page 1 shows that there were five hundred towns about the size of a couple of average comprehensive schools. Another fifty had populations going up to around 5,000. All 550 or so were market towns which also had a church and its clerygymen, a meeting place for magistrates and homes for professional people such as lawyers and doctors. You would also find a dozen or so skilled craftsmen: masons, carpenters, saddlers, bakers and tailors. Unlike the handworkers in Units 1A and 1B such men did most of the work on a product from start to finish. Many would have an apprentice whose family had paid for him to be taught the trade over seven years starting at 12 or 14 years of age.

Merchant centres

There were fifteen towns with more than 7,000 people. Most were centres for the manufactures of the countryside around. In Norwich, Exeter and Colchester you would find merchant clothiers' homes, warehouses and the cloth hall. Sometimes there were small workshops like the fulling mills and dye-houses in Exeter. But many of its 12,000 people had jobs not directly concerned with cloth making. They were warehousemen, packhorse and waggon drivers, merchants' clerks as well as the shopkeepers and craftsmen you would find in a market town. In addition, Exeter had many inns used mostly by travellers connected with the woollen trades. In 1696 they could shelter 866 guests and 1,037 horses.

Manchester was becoming a centre for buying and selling cloth. But its few thousand people lived inside a quarter-square-mile. Birmingham was a centre for iron-masters who owned forges and slitting mills in the countryside around. Its inns were business places where iron-mongers made their deals to buy bars or rods from the masters. The same inns often stored the iron-mongers' goods while they were waiting for waggons.

Seaports

Seaports such as Bristol and Glasgow combined trading and manufacturing. Apart from merchants and their warehouse clerks and labourers, there were ship-builders, sail-makers and rope-makers. Other trades arose from imported goods. Glasgow had workshops where tobacco was cured and rolled into cigars. In Bristol, brown sticky sugar from the West Indies was boiled into white crystals. One by-product was rum which was sent back to America and the West Indies in bottles made in Bristol. In the 1720s there were fifteen glasshouses. Yet the refineries, glasshouses and tobacco-curing shops usually had only a dozen or so workers each.

London

London held about one in twelve of all people in England. It was the centre of government, the law and the church and of high society, so many landowners had a second home there. London was the busiest port for products made all over Britain so it was the headquarters of many merchants and owners of waggon businesses. Large numbers worked in the warehouses, on the quay sides, in ship-building yards or rope- and sail-making workshops. It was also a manufacturing town. To the east was Spitalfields, a centre for silk weaving started by Huguenots who were Protestant refugees from Catholic France. Thousands of weavers worked in their own homes on materials supplied by silk merchants.

Because of the number of wealthy people, London became a great centre for the service trades. While market towns might have a single tailor and joiner, London had hundreds, as well as tradesmen you would find nowhere else such as coach-builders.

C   Handworking in towns

C1   A turner making furniture with the help of a pole lathe worked with his feet.

C2   A brickmaker putting clay into moulds before baking.

6. Suggest what were
   a) the similarities and
   b) the differences
   between these workers and those in the main manufactures such as wool and iron.

D ENERGY, POWER AND TECHNOLOGY

Energy for power

Most of the energy used in manufacturing around 1700 came from human muscles. They turned the spinning-wheel, threw the shuttle across the loom, hammered the nail or hacked away at the coal.

The most useful alternatives were wind- and water-mills. Windmills were an ancient way of turning wheels to grind corn or lift water out of marshy areas. But wind was an unreliable source of power. Water power was available all winter and even longer if you built a mill-pond to store it for summer. It could turn grindstones and work bellows, or trip hammers which fell down on to a lump of metal or a length of cloth in a fulling trough.

A

A windmill turning a wheel which lifted water from the fens.

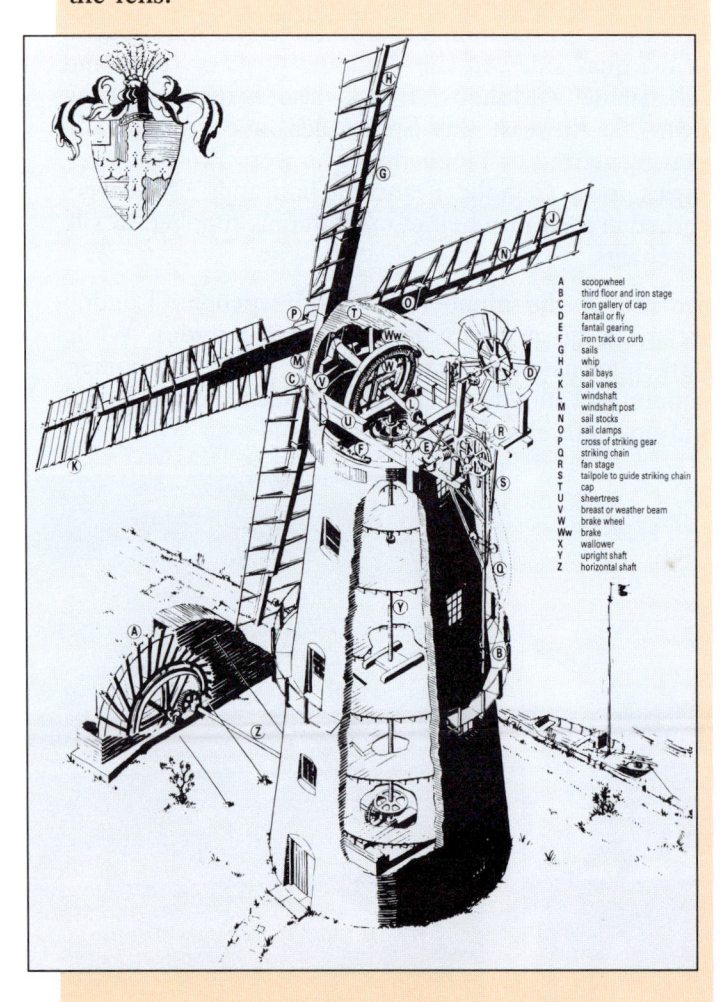

A	scoopwheel
B	third floor and iron stage
C	iron gallery of cap
D	fantail or fly
E	fantail gearing
F	iron track or curb
G	sails
H	whip
I	sail bays
J	sail vanes
K	sail stocks
L	windshaft
M	windshaft post
N	sail clamps
O	cross of striking gear
P	striking chain
Q	fan stage
R	tailpole to guide striking chain
S	cap
T	sheertrees
U	breast or weather beam
V	brake wheel
W	brake
Ww	wallower
X	upright shaft
Y	
Z	horizontal shaft

For some tasks, animal power was more helpful. Dogs were used to turn spits in large kitchens. Horses gave more power and could be made to work whenever they were needed. One of the most common uses was the whim-gin where a horse was led round in a circle to wind up men or baskets of coal from a pit.

B

A eighteenth-century diagram showing how water-power could work bellows.

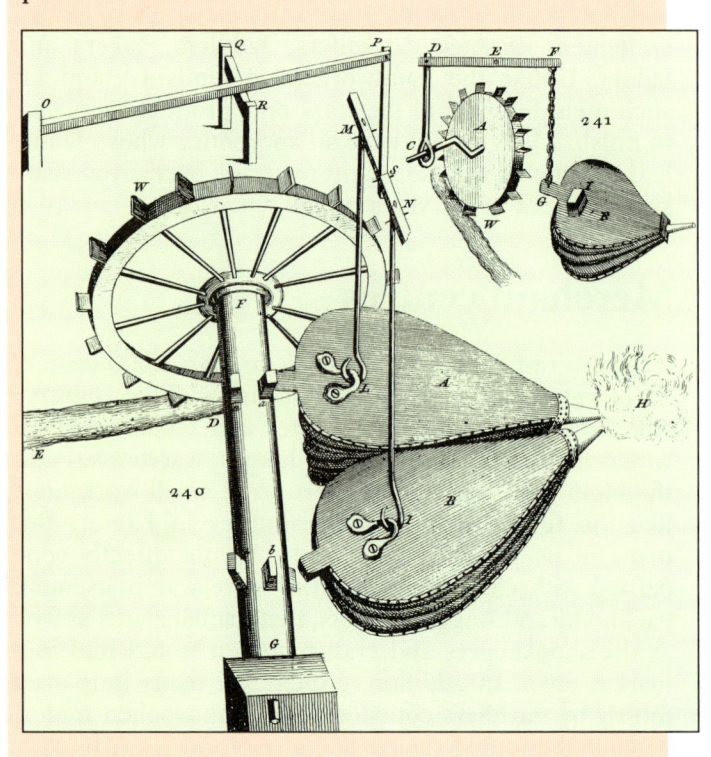

Energy for heating

Many manufacturing tasks needed heat: soap-making, dyeing and washing, iron-working and brewing. The traditional fuel was wood (or charcoal) but by 1700 coal was being used in many places. The total in 1700 was 2½ million tons, about half of what can be used in a single power station. To bring this up required about 15,000 workers across Britain. In most places there were no more than a dozen or so to one pit, sometimes only a man with his wife or children to take away the coal. Many pits were circular holes in the ground known as bell pits but there were others where a mineshaft was sunk and the miners dug passages from its bottom to the coalface.

The biggest number of these mines were in the Northumberland and Durham coalfield. Sometimes there would be thirty to forty workers, usually working in gangs. At its head was the hewer who cut the coal in his stall, which was a space between pillars of coal left to keep the mine roof up. He paid a gang of women and children, including his own, to drag the corves, or baskets of coal, along the mine passages to the bottom of the shaft. Here they were wound to the surface by a whim-gin.

Nearly all the coal from these pits found its way to London. It was first loaded onto flat-bottomed keels at Newcastle to be carried out to waiting coal-ships. Once

C

A whim-gin at a coal-mine.

1. From this picture of a coal-mine can you explain how the whim-gin worked?

they had delivered the 'sea-coal' to London some of it was used for heating homes and the rest went to the city's many breweries, soap-works, dye-houses and other workplaces.

Gears and wheels

All the forms of capturing energy by wind, water or animal power had one thing in common. They could not have worked without the rods, gears and wheels which transmitted the energy to where it was needed. This meant that the skill of gear-makers, wheel-cutters and the people who put the parts together were vital to all heavy manufacturing and mining work. Most of these driving parts were made of wood but in some cases small amounts of special metals were needed. You saw in Unit 1B how slitting mills had steel to slice the bars into rods. For other parts brass was used.

Steel and brass could only be made in tiny quantities at a time. The aim of the steel-maker was to produce a metal which had some bend in it but was also hard so it could be used for the edge of cutting tools and for making springs. He did this by heating slices of bar iron and charcoal together in a clay pot for several days. The result was 'blister' steel, so called because of the appearance of its surface. Brass was a mixture of copper and zinc. The two were placed together in fireclay pots, heated until they mixed together as liquid and then poured into sand or stone moulds of the shape the brass-founder wanted.

A lot of the understanding of the mechanisms which drove windmills and water-wheels came from the ancient trade of clockmaking. Clockmaking was one of the first manufactures to have any kind of machine-tool – a machine which can shape the parts needed in other machines.

Clockmaking may have used finer metals and more precisely-made parts but it was no different from other trades, such as textiles, in any important way. The work was usually broken down into different stages.

D

A clockmaker's wheel cutting machine, about 1762.

2. What do machines A to D have in common?
3. Which sources of energy can you identify?

E

An account of watch making.

> The movement-maker forges his wheels...sends them to the cutter and has them cut at a trifling expense. He has nothing to do when he takes them from the cutter but to finish them and turn the corners of the teeth. The pinions made of steel are drawn at the mills so the watchmaker has only to file down the points...The springs are made by a tradesman who does nothing else, and the chains by another. The last are frequently made by women...There are workmen who make nothing else but the caps and studs for watches...
>
> R. Campbell, *The London Tradesmen*, 1747

E SKILLS SECTION

Using sources

It would be impossible to follow the account of manufacturing in this part without studying the many different kinds of eighteenth-century sources that have been used. These sources could be broken down into the list below. Complete the table:

Type of source	Examples in Part 1	What can be learned from the source
Newspapers		
Memoirs		
Travel books		
Paintings		
Technical illustrations		
Personal letters		
Advertisements		

1. From the written sources, what do you notice about eighteenth-century rules of grammar?
2. From the picture sources which do you think were engravings and which were water colours? What was the difference between the way the artists worked?
3. Which written source did you find a) most difficult, and b) easiest to understand? Explain why.
4. Which of the picture sources do you think may have given a) the least accurate, and b) the most accurate evidence about its subject. Explain your choices.

Word meanings

History is a lot easier to study if you can understand the meanings given to words by people of the time.

Complete this chart.

Word	Eighteenth-century meaning	Has the meaning changed?
carding		
calico		
clothier		
fulling		
fustian		
'gin		
industry		
knitter		
knitting frame		
manufacturing		
sea-island cotton		
warp		
weft		
yarn		

Knowledge and understanding

1. About a hundred years ago a historian used the term 'domestic system' to describe the kind of manufacturing that went on in the early eighteenth century. List three ways in which what you know about the work and the workers makes this a good description.
2. Later historians have often written about the ways in which eighteenth-century manufacturing was run on capitalist lines as most industry and trade is today. Give three examples which might support this view.
3. In which ways did eighteenth-century working women a) have, and b) not have 'equal opportunities' with men?

Before you read on:

Most of the descriptions in Part One have been taken from the first twenty or so years of the eighteenth century. Some of them come from the middle years of the century because the traditional ways of working did not die out suddenly. However, from the 1720s there was a growing number of changes in working methods as well as many new inventions. Part Two describes the most important of these changes.

2

1700s–1780s: IMPROVERS AND INVENTERS

How manufacturing came out of the cottage into the workshop, helped by improvements in transport.

- A Cotton speeds up
- B Iron: the development of scale and skill
- C Transport and manufacturing
- D Technology and manufacturing
- E Overseas trade and banking
- F Skills section: reading an eighteenth-century writer

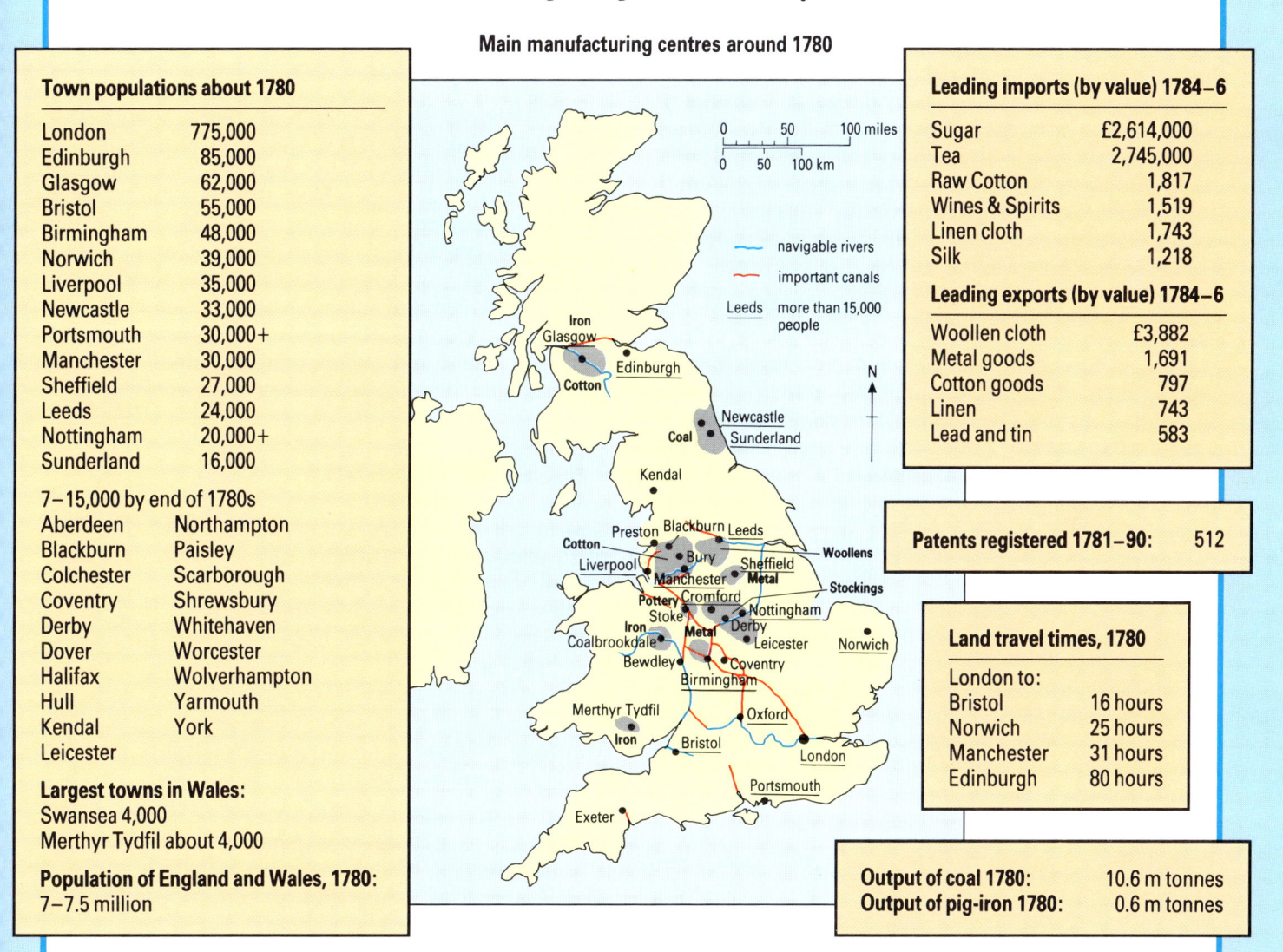

Main manufacturing centres around 1780

Town populations about 1780

London	775,000
Edinburgh	85,000
Glasgow	62,000
Bristol	55,000
Birmingham	48,000
Norwich	39,000
Liverpool	35,000
Newcastle	33,000
Portsmouth	30,000+
Manchester	30,000
Sheffield	27,000
Leeds	24,000
Nottingham	20,000+
Sunderland	16,000

7–15,000 by end of 1780s

Aberdeen	Northampton
Blackburn	Paisley
Colchester	Scarborough
Coventry	Shrewsbury
Derby	Whitehaven
Dover	Worcester
Halifax	Wolverhampton
Hull	Yarmouth
Kendal	York
Leicester	

Largest towns in Wales:
Swansea 4,000
Merthyr Tydfil about 4,000

Population of England and Wales, 1780:
7–7.5 million

Leading imports (by value) 1784–6

Sugar	£2,614,000
Tea	2,745,000
Raw Cotton	1,817
Wines & Spirits	1,519
Linen cloth	1,743
Silk	1,218

Leading exports (by value) 1784–6

Woollen cloth	£3,882
Metal goods	1,691
Cotton goods	797
Linen	743
Lead and tin	583

Patents registered 1781–90: 512

Land travel times, 1780

London to:	
Bristol	16 hours
Norwich	25 hours
Manchester	31 hours
Edinburgh	80 hours

Output of coal 1780: 10.6 m tonnes
Output of pig-iron 1780: 0.6 m tonnes

Before you read on:

a) Compare this information with page 1. How would you describe the changes in: town size; overseas trade; travel times; output of iron and coal?
b) Can you see any connections between these changes?
c) What does the change in the number of patents suggest?
d) Do your answers to **a** to **c** suggest any reasons why a canal system was developing by the 1780s?

11

A COTTON SPEEDS UP

Britain was a sheep-raising country and making woollen cloth was its oldest branch of textiles. In the eighteenth century, raw cotton was a new raw material which attracted men trying to find new openings for marketing their goods. As we saw in Unit 1B, Nottingham hosiers challenged silk and wool stocking-makers with their cotton hose while Lancashire clothiers used cotton in fustian as a cheap alternative to linen and calico. To increase their sales these new masters would encourage anyone who could find ways of speeding up production and cutting the wages paid to handworkers.

The workshop inventions

In 1733 a Lancashire loom mechanic, James Kay from Bury, invented the flying shuttle. On a loom the warp threads were fixed top to bottom and the weaver passed a shuttle carrying a spool of weft thread through them. For anything but the narrowest cloth he needed an assistant to do this. With Kay's invention he could send the shuttle flying along a runner when he jerked a cord. It met with a cool reception from weavers angry at a machine which could halve the number of workers. They wrecked Kay's home and he fled to France.

Within twenty years the flying shuttle was becoming standard, helped by John Kay's son who added a drop box to hold several shuttles each with a different colour. Around then, in 1755, a hosier in Derby, Jeddediah Strutt, had invented the ribbing frame. This made a tough cotton stocking which did not need seaming by hand. To safeguard the early models he put the frames in a room with skylights but no windows.

Faster weaving and more stocking knitting created a need for a way of making more yarn without having to employ thousands of extra cottage spinners. There had been an attempt in 1738 when Lewis Paul used the help of an inventor, John Wyatt, to build a roller-spinner. The idea was that the thread would be drawn out if you passed the cotton through two rollers, one moving faster than the other. He tried it first in a Birmingham workshop and then moved to Nottingham to supply the hosiery business. He failed because he never got his machine to work without technical hiccups.

In the 1750s a Lancashire farmer, Robert Peel, set up in a second business as a cotton clothier. He encouraged a Blackburn mechanic, James Hargreaves to study ways of speeding up spinning. In about 1764 Hargreaves came up with a design for making one handle turn eight spindles which was so simple that a child could work it. As well as 'gin', another everyday word for machines or engines was 'jenny' and Hargreaves' contraption became the 'spinning jenny'.

The jenny was no more popular than the flying shuttle. In 1768 cottage workers wrecked the barn where Hargreaves was building twenty jennies. He left for Nottingham and opened a workshop with jennies but they could not spin yarn fine enough for the local knitters. But back in Lancashire, the jenny led to a tremendous rise in the amount of weft threads for fustian. Models with side handles, which meant one adult could turn twenty spindles, were soon being built.

Into the workshop

Flying-shuttle looms, rib-frames and jennies could all be used in the home but they could not be bought at prices which handworkers could afford. Master clothiers or hosiers bought a few at a time and put them into a workshop. They could keep an eye on production and take on weavers, spinners or knitters who agreed to do a six-day week without Saint Monday. The workshop could be situated near to fulling mills, dye-sheds or cotton-printing shops.

Some masters took on 'pauper apprentices' who were orphan girls and boys aged ten or so. Such children were the responsibility of the poor law officer in each parish. They used money from the poor rates to find them lodgings and training to earn their own living. Some poor law officers began to pay fees to master clothiers to take on these children. In fact they were to become unskilled and unpaid labourers, although they were called 'apprentices' because the master agreed to give them board and lodgings in the same way that a craftsman did when he took a boy as an apprentice.

The spinning mill

New inventions and workshop methods meant a speed up in manufacturing fustians and stockings. But there was still a vital material missing. The jenny made cotton which was strong enough for the weft threads in fustian but it snapped when weavers tried to use it for warp to make all-cotton goods. Nor was it strong enough for stocking frames. There was plenty of talk about this problem and it must have been heard by Richard Arkwright who had done two jobs for talkative people – as a barber and a salesman for a wig-maker.

Arkwright decided to go back to Paul's idea of a roller-spinner and got a local clockmaker to make the parts. The first working model was finished in 1768, the year when Hargreaves' home was wrecked. Arkwright took no chances and carried his roller-spinner to Nottingham. Here he interested Jeddediah Strutt and another manufacturer in the idea. They put up the money for a large-scale version in a workshop where it was driven by a wheel turned by horses. It worked well and produced thread strong enough for stocking frames but there was something else. Arkwright had hit on a major advance in textile manufacture. The spinner no longer needed to turn a wheel. The machine did that. All it needed were large numbers of minders to tie or 'piece' threads when they snapped and to change full spindles for empty ones.

Separating the worker and the power was not completely new. Back in 1719, John and Thomas Lombe had copied an Italian machine for 'throwing' silk into thread. They had built a mill on the River Derwent in Derbyshire where 300 women attended to the silk reels which were turned by water-wheel. Other silk mills had been built and this led Jeddediah Strutt to suggest to Arkwright that he should try water power. In 1771 he had a four-storey building built at Cromford in Derbyshire. One water-wheel drove enough spindles to employ 'about 200 workers, mostly children'. From then, his invention was known as the 'water-frame'.

Arkwright built around twenty mills, mostly in Pennine valleys. In Scotland he went into partnership with David Dale to open the New Lanark mills in a valley southwest of Glasgow. Other men copied him so that by 1788 there were 143 Arkwright-type mills, mostly in the midlands. There were few in Lancashire where most spinning was done by around 20,000 jennies. But workshop owners there were turning to another invention by a Bolton man, Samuel Crompton. He called it a mule because it was a cross between a jenny and a frame.

The mule

In many ways the mule was the most important invention of all. It spun thread strong enough for warp so that fustian quickly gave way to all-cotton goods. It worked more spindles than the jenny. It could be built in different sizes according to the space in the workshop and there was a choice of hand or water power. It was the ideal piece of equipment for the small master who could not afford to build a mill. With the mule to back up the jenny, the lonely cottage spinner making cotton or linen thread soon became a figure of the past.

A Reconstructions of spinning machines

A1 Quarry Bank, Cheshire. The Spinning Jenny rebuilt from Hargreaves's patent in 1770.

A2 Helmshore Museum, Lancashire. A ninety-six spindle water frame from Arkwright's mill at Cromford. The wooden drum between the two halves drives them with power from the water-wheel.

A3 Ghent Museum, Belgium. A reconstruction of a thirty frame mule smuggled out of Britain in 1790. At that time it was illegal to export machinery which would help overseas competitors.

1. How would you describe the differences between the jenny and the frame from a) the workers' and b) the masters' point of view?
2. Does the 1790's mule suggest anything about changes in machine-making skills from the time of the 1770's frame?

B IRON: THE DEVELOPMENT OF SKILL AND SCALE

Changes in the iron trades began like those in textiles with the search for new products to sell. Abraham Darby was born in the midlands but had gone to Bristol to join a firm which cast brass into ornaments and small machine parts. He worked out a way of using a blast furnace to cast iron goods by letting the liquid metal run into moulds instead of pigs. The possibility of mass-producing everyday objects such as cooking pots led him back to the midlands to Coalbrookdale on the River Severn. There were coal and iron in pits nearby and a stream to work the bellows for the furnace. The River Severn would carry goods to the sea.

In 1709, Darby improved the heat in the furnace by using coal instead of charcoal. Earlier men had failed to do this because the sulphur in coal ruined the metal but Darby first turned it into coke by cooking it in a heap under wet ashes. Soon Coalbrookdale pots, fireback plates, iron railings and so on were in great demand.

Abraham Darby died in 1717. In turn his son-in-law, (Richard Ford), his son and grandson (Abraham Darby II and III) ran the business until 1789. They developed a second reputation for Coalbrookdale as the place which could supply iron parts to the changing technology of the times. Richard Ford made cylinders and pistons for Newcomen's atmospheric, or 'fire', engine for pumping water (see Unit 2D). Cast-iron cylinders could be several times larger than brass ones. To do this Richard Ford had to build workshops where the cylinders were bored smooth by water-driven machinery.

Other iron-masters were slow to copy the Darbys' coke-fired furnaces. Then the Seven Years War (1756–63) brought a great demand for cannon, cannon-balls and bullets (which the Darbys would not make because they were Quakers). English iron-masters moved into south Wales, to Merthyr Tydfil, where a few families divided their time between sheep farming and digging coal from shallow mines. It became the fastest growing district of Britain. By 1765 there were four large iron-works. In Scotland, John Roebuck and two partners opened the Carron works near Falkirk in 1759. They recruited

A

A Darby contribution to new technology.

A fire engine cylinder was landed at Wincomblee coal staith on the river Tyne for the use of Walker Colliery, which surpassed everything of the kind that had been seen in the North. The diameter of the bore measured upwards of 74 inches and it was 10½ feet in length. Its weight exclusive of the bottom and the piston, was 6½ tons containing altogether between 10 and 11 tons of metal. The bore was perfectly round and well polished. It was considered a complete piece of work and did honour to Coalbrookdale foundry in Shropshire.

Quoted in M.A. Richardson,
The Local Historian's Table Book, 1842

1. What does this tell you about the skill of Coalbrookdale workmen as a) iron-casters and b) engineers?
2. How would the cylinder have reached the Walker Colliery?

B

Coalbrookdale in 1758, with a cylinder being taken to the river.

3. Find: (from left to right) the pumping house which used a Newcomen steam-pump, two blast furnaces, piles of coal being coked.

skilled workers from Coalbrookdale. So did John Wilkinson who opened several iron-works in Shropshire and Staffordshire.

These iron-masters all used coke which took the weight of a lot more iron ore than charcoal, so the furnaces were larger. All the new works depended on engineering skills. They made huge iron blowing-cylinders, powered by water-wheels, to blast air into their furnaces. Other water-wheels drove grinding and boring machines which smoothed their cannon and other products. As more iron poured from the furnaces the masters began to look for new uses. John 'iron-mad' Wilkinson, made water pipes as well as one of the first iron boats. He and the Darbys made iron plateways for carts to run along and pioneered the use of iron girders for building. In 1779 Abraham Darby III cast all the parts for the world's first all-iron bridge over the River Severn.

The handworkers

While the iron-masters were making their huge products, changes were taking place among the handworkers. Just as in textiles, many jobs were taken into workshops to make use of new inventions. Sheffield became the centre for the finest cutting tools. There were thirty-eight employers with workshops making 'fine scissors' and thirteen who made surgeon's lancets and phlemes (for bloodletting). It was also a centre for high quality steel used for springs and levers for watches as well as the cutting edges of lathes and other machine-tools. All this began with a watchmaker, Benjamin Huntsman, who was dissatisfied with the old blister steel. After years of experiment he made his first 'crucible steel' in 1746. It was a rediscovery of a method of the ancient Chinese and Indians who put a small amount of hammered iron in a clay crucible and heated it white-hot in a charcoal furnace.

While the town became a centre for high quality goods, the countryside around held the cottages and small forges of handworkers in the less skilled branches of the cutlery trade – 'common scissors', pen and pocket knives, razors and files. The same was true of Birmingham. Outside the city, there were a dozen villages where handworkers turned out nails and other objects as they had done fifty years earlier. Inside the town there had been great changes.

In 1700 Birmingham had been a base for iron merchants and iron-mongers, not for manufacturing. By the 1760s it was flourishing in the toy trade – small metal goods, such as clocks, buckles, buttons, snuff boxes, locks, and ornamental plates. It was a place of workshops where men and women used small furnaces to cast fine quality iron or brass parts. They worked with many new inventions such as metal-turning lathes and hand-worked machines which could press metal shapes or stamp out coins, medals, snuff-box lids and so on.

Some workshops had more than a hundred workers but none was as large as Soho Manufactory which Matthew Boulton opened in 1762. He started as a buckle manufacturer and moved into many other branches of the toy trade as well as making coins. The Soho Manufactory had between 700 and 800 men, women and children employees and must have been the largest workplace in Britain. Yet it was really a collection of dozens of workshops under the same roof. In each one you could see the effects of machines which were changing the metal trades as the jenny and mule changed textiles.

C

Inside a workshop in the Soho Manufactory.

> When a Man stamps on a metal Button by means of an Engine, a Child stands by him to place the Button in readiness to receive the Stamp and to remove it when received and then to place another. By these Means the Operator can stamp at least double the Number, which he could otherwise have done... at the same time that it trains up Children to an Habit of Industry, almost as soon as they can speak.

Josiah Tucker, *Manifold Causes of the Increase of the Poor*, 1760

4. What does Josiah Tucker mean by 'an Engine' and 'Industry'?
5. Does the passage give any evidence about general eighteenth-century attitudes to children's work?

D

A Birmingham shop in the late eighteenth century.

6. What does this suggest about workshop manufacturing in Birmingham?
7. List the objects you can identify the use of.

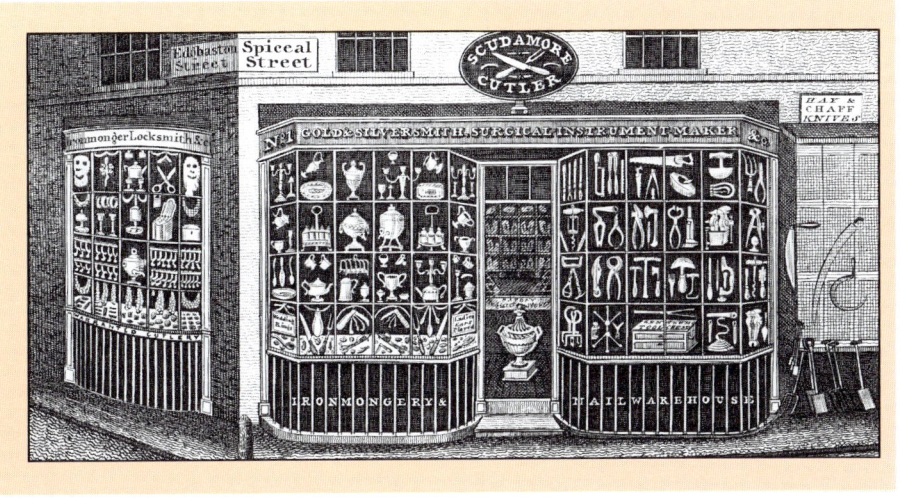

15

C TRANSPORT AND MANUFACTURING

A

Josiah Wedgwood's new works at Etruria, near Stoke-on-Trent in 1769.

1. What does this tell you about the connection between transport and manufacturing?

Wedgwood called his works 'Etruria' after the Etruscan style of some of his pottery which was becoming famous in many parts of Europe. When Wedgwood was a boy the pottery industry of the Stoke-on-Trent district was a small-scale affair turning out mostly earthenware jugs, cups and plates. He became the leading figure in a group of pottery owners who were trying to bring their products up-market. His company bought fine white clay from Cornwall, opened salesrooms in London and Liverpool and sent samples of porcelain abroad. Above all, Wedgwood revolutionised the way that pottery-making was organised. Like his friend, Matthew Boulton at the Soho Manufactory, he divided Etruria into workshops where workers, usually only semi-skilled, concentrated on a separate stage in making his pottery.

Wedgwood's biggest problem was transport. The pottery district was in the middle of England far from the sea. Yet it needed large loads of china clay from Cornwall, which were combined with powder made by grinding tonnes of flints brought from south-east England. Its products were sent out in crates, thickly wrapped in straw to cut down breakages.

Road carriers

Transport problems such as these had been greatly helped by the road improvements carried out by the Turnpike Trusts, mostly from the 1720s onwards. The Trusts collected tolls from road users to pay for repairs to the road surfaces. From a manufacturer's point of view the most important result was that the major routes between towns became firm enough to bear the weight of waggons pulled by six or eight horses. At the beginning of the eighteenth century, there had been few waggons on the roads and most of them had to give up work in the winter when roads were quagmires of mud. In 1762 when Matthew Boulton built the Soho Manufactory, he was able to make sure of regular supplies by putting it at the side of the turnpike road which led to the coal and iron districts.

Turnpike roads led to the setting up of many carrier businesses. Some moved goods in bulk for a man such as Boulton but many others ran stage-waggon services carrying anything which was delivered to them. The waggons covered regular routes at announced times. Each stage ended at an inn which was a sort of combined motel and warehouse. The waggoner could get a meal or a night's rest and have his horses changed. He loaded goods waiting there and off-loaded some to be collected by customers or put on a stage-waggon going in a different direction. The carrier services provided the first regular link between the towns of Britain, apart from post-boys carrying letters on horseback.

B

Weekly carrier links from Newcastle, 1788.

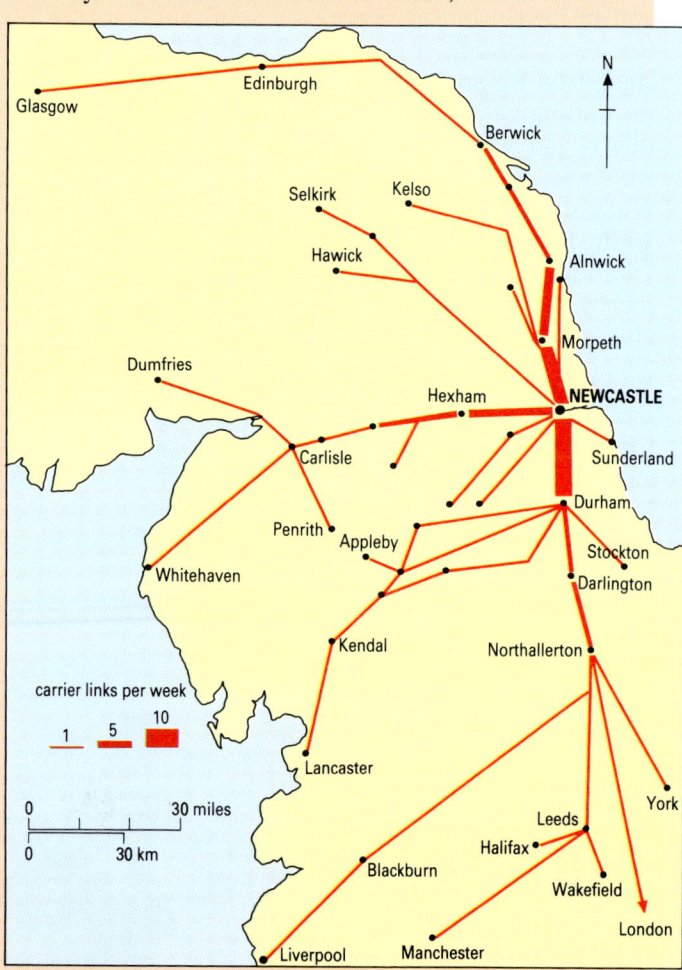

2. These services would have been impossible thirty years earlier. In which ways would they have been a help to manufacturers of the 1780s?

Turnpikes eased the transport problems of the pottery district. Three weekly waggons went to Bridgenorth or Bewdley on the River Severn with eight tonnes of pottery which went down to Bristol. They made the return journey with ten tonnes of white clay and other goods. Other waggons made similar trips to the River Weaver which was linked with the Mersey and Liverpool or went about the same distance to the nearest place where the River Trent was navigable. From there pots went down-river to Hull, and up came the flints which had travelled to Hull by sea from Kent.

The cost of all this was high and the risk of damage to pottery was great. It is not at all surprising that Josiah Wedgwood was quick to see the possibilities for his business when James Brindley built Britain's first cross-country canal for the Duke of Bridgwater in 1761. It was only twelve miles long but it carried coal from the Duke's mines to Manchester so cheaply that he could cut the price in half. Josiah Wedgwood set about collecting names of people who would become shareholders in a new canal which would link the rivers Trent and Mersey and then have other canals running down to the River Severn and into Birmingham.

C

C1 A letter from Josiah Wedgwood.

> The present price of freight and carriage of clay and flint for pottery in Staffordshire which is 15/– per Ton on average, will be reduced by this new conveyance to 2/– per Ton on about 4000 Tons which are sent up annually; and the carriage and freight of the Earthenware in return, will be reduced from 28/– to about 12/– per Ton, which must greatly increase the exportation of that manufacture from this Port.
>
> *Josiah Wedgwood in Liverpool,* 16 May 1765

C2

One horse could pull:
on soft roads ⅛ ton
on a surfaced turnpike road ¼ ton
on wooden rails 2 tons
on metal rails 10 tons
on a canal 30 tons

3. Suggest why Wedgwood expected the cost of moving his raw materials to fall more than the charges for moving his pottery.
4. How does table C2 help to explain the cheaper price of canal transport? What other reasons can you think of?

Brindley was hired to take charge of building the Trent & Mersey and its first important branches such as the Staffordshire & Worcestershire Canal which ran into the River Severn. It was the start of a network which, in twenty years, linked all the major towns and manufacturing centres. For the five pottery towns in the middle of England the results were just as Wedgwood hoped.

The pottery business boomed and the population rose from 7,000 in 1760 to 21,000 in 1785. The results were even more dramatic in Birmingham which became the centre of what Brindley called a 'silver cross'.

Matthew Boulton was described as 'one of the most active promoters' of the Birmingham Canal which ran through the same iron and coal districts as the turnpike road he had used earlier. It passed half a mile from the Soho works so he built his own branch canal to join it. In the rest of the town the banks of the canal were soon lined with new workshops and warehouses. The canal-side became the favoured spot for new manufactures just as industrial sites are placed near motorways today.

D

Birmingham:

Population	Canal links
1750: 25,000	
1760: 31,000	1769 – Birmingham Canal to Staffordshire iron and coal
1770: 43,000	1772 – Birmingham Canal extended to give route to Severn
	1777 – Fazely Canal links with Mersey & Trent to Liverpool and Hull
1780: 50,000	1789 – Shorter link to Mersey & Trent
1790: 60,000	1790 – Link with London via Oxford Canal
	1799 – Direct link with London via Grand Union canal.
1801: 74,000	

5. How does this chart help to explain what Brindley meant by a 'silver cross'?
6. What does the chart suggest about the connection between canals, manufacturing and population.

Waggonways

There was one other important means of shifting heavy goods over shorter distances. This was the waggonway laid for horses to pull carts of coal or iron ore as far as the nearest water. The first waggonways had been flat strips of wood laid over the ground. Later an iron plate was laid on top of the wood and in 1767 the Darby works at Coalbrookdale made the first cast-iron rails which were laid across 'sleepers' of wood or stone. In the next four years they made 800 tonnes of these rails and soon other iron-masters turned them out whenever their furnaces had little other work. In the mining district of Northumberland and Durham there were dozens of these private waggonways built by mine-owners to carry their coal to barges on the River Tyne. In the 1790s, when canals were built from the Welsh coast to the ironworks at Merthyr Tydfil, there were more miles of waggonway then canal.

D TECHNOLOGY AND MANUFACTURING

Water power

In 1727 a traveller noted that 'overshot mills are becoming most general (especially in the northern parts of England)'. It was an important change. Most earlier water-wheels were undershot. The lower part of the wheel was in a stream which forced it to spin upwards. The overshot wheel was set in a trough and turned by water pouring from above, which made a more powerful movement. The wheel need not be on the banks of a stream provided that the workshop owner could afford to have a channel built to carry water to it.

Every district had its skilled millwrights who could take charge of setting up a new wheel. They might employ dozens of workers such as masons to build the channels, wheelwrights and clockmakers which was a common term for those who cut the gear wheels and fitted them together so that a slowly turning water-wheel could spin a grindstone, a jenny, a mule or a boring machine.

A

Employment for Clock-Makers...Robinson and Walmesley, Pall Mall, Manchester. N.B. Would be more agreeable if they have been before employed in Cotton Works.

Manchester Mercury, 23 July 1782

B

Wheelwright at work.

By the 1750s and 1760s some manufacturers were asking for more power. When Matthew Boulton opened the Soho Manufactory he had just two water-wheels to drive the machinery used by 600 workers. Arkwright had one wheel for his three-storied mill. There were often several water-wheels at ironworks such as John Wilkinson's or the Carron works in Scotland because much horse-power was needed to blow the blast into a large coke-fired furnace or to turn a boring machine.

The problem interested one of the greatest engineers of the time, John Smeaton (1724–92). He carried out experiments to measure the power you could get from different kinds of water-wheel and showed that the best results came with a breast-shot wheel. The water was forced through a narrow channel and aimed at just one section of the top half of the wheel.

C

Breast-shot wheel.

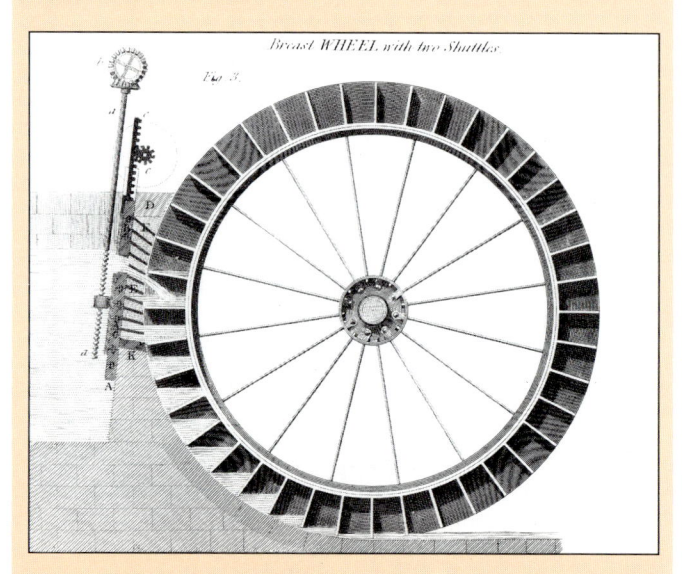

A Rees, *The Cyclopaedia, or Universal Dictionary of Arts, Sciences, and Literature*, 1819

1. What was the purpose of the screw arrangement on the left?

One of the places which Smeaton advised on water-power was the Carron ironworks. He interested them in making cast-iron parts for the water-wheel itself and for the rods and gears which drove the machinery. By the time that he died, a Smeaton-type water-wheel was a long way from the primitive wooden contraption that had turned corn-mills for centuries. It might produce 80 horse-power or more, and keep a large factory going as this sketch of one of the Strutt cotton-mills shows.

Machine technology

Cast-iron was important not only for water-wheels. The skill of the caster lay behind the many changes in engineering which were vital to the new large-scale production in both metal and textiles. One of the most important new pieces of equipment was the boring machine which smoothed the barrels of cannon and the inside of cylinders. But many humbler cast-iron machines were made. One was the cutting engine which clockmakers used on site to cut the gears. A large mill needed a clockmakers' shop where repairs were carried out and a cutting engine was usually a standard piece of equipment.

D

Belper Mill.

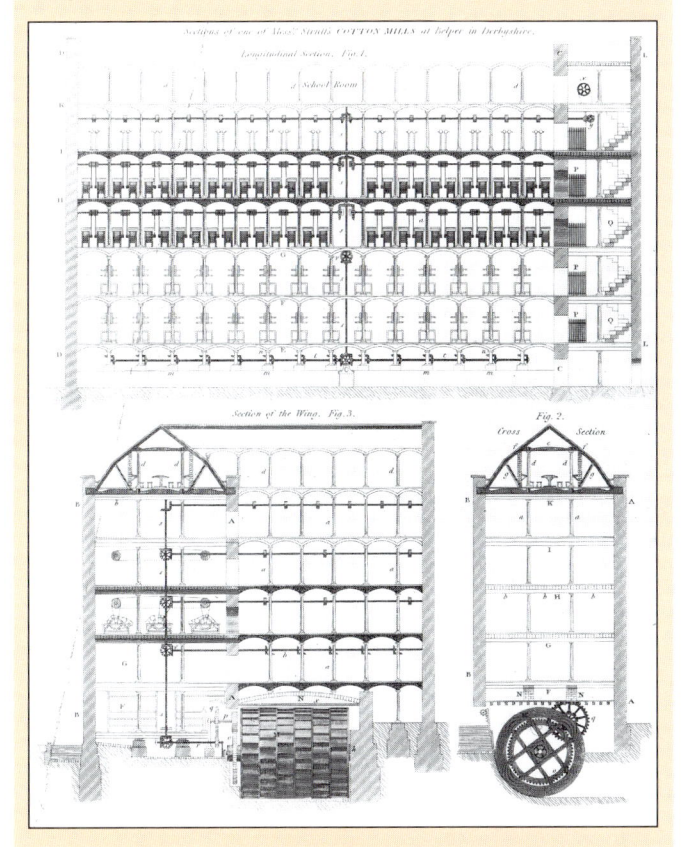

A Rees, *The Cyclopaedia*, 1819

2. What was the author of the *Cyclopaedia* trying to show with this diagram?

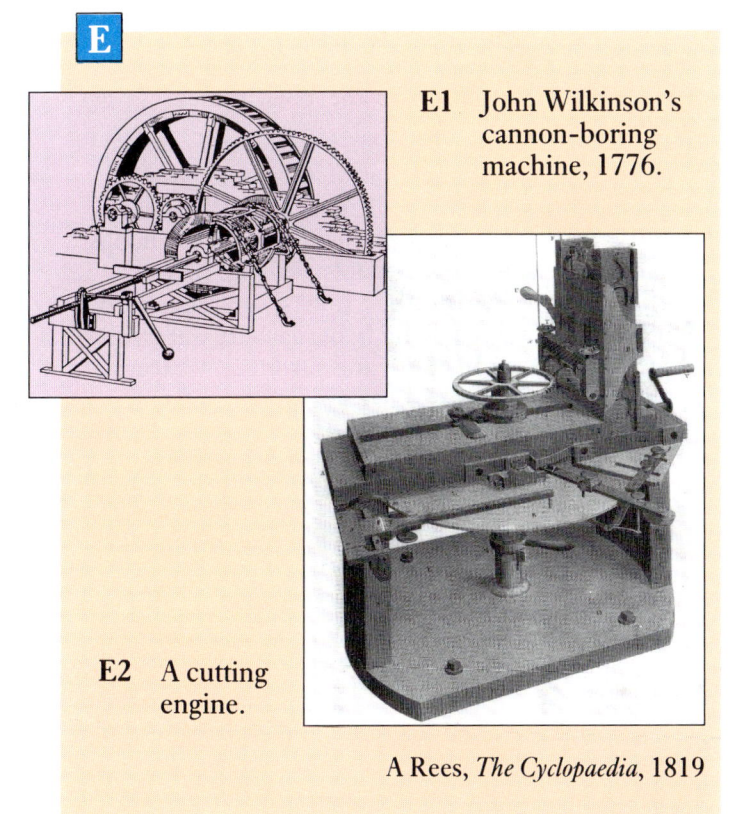

E

E1 John Wilkinson's cannon-boring machine, 1776.

E2 A cutting engine.

A Rees, *The Cyclopaedia*, 1819

3. What material are both these machines made of?

Steam power

By the 1770s there were over 200 steam engines but no-one thought of them as a means of bringing power to machinery. They were 'atmospheric' engines for pumping water. The first had been built in 1712 by Thomas Newcomen to pump water from Cornish tin-mines. Most of it could be built on the spot by carpenters, bricklayers and blacksmiths. Steam from the boiler pushed a piston up a cylinder. As it came up, the beam on top tilted to make the down-stroke of the pump. The cylinder was then cooled with water, the steam condensed and the pressure of the atmosphere forced the piston down pulling the beam to make the up-stroke.

F

An eighteenth-century demonstration model of the Newcomen engine preserved in the Science Museum.

4. Make a rough sketch and label it to show how the engine worked.

Newcomen engines used so much coal that they were too expensive for Cornish mine-owners who had to pay for it to be delivered by sea. Instead they spread through the coal-mining districts. A quarter of the cost would go on the cylinder and piston. The first were made of brass and reached about 75 cm diameter. Later ones were cast-iron, mostly from Coalbrookdale, and could be over twice that size. Another important use for Newcomen engines was to lift water into mill-ponds to drive water-wheels. But until 1783 this was the only link between steam power and machinery.

E OVERSEAS TRADE AND BANKING

In 1700 the greatest part of Britain's trade was with Europe. By the 1780s this was no longer true.

Trading to the west and east

In 1783 the United States won their freedom from Britain but their 2½ million white people still had strong trade links with her. There were another half million in British-owned West Indian islands and Canada, as well as more than a million African slaves in the West Indies and the USA. This added up to 4 million people to be supplied with British goods on top of the 7½ million already in Britain.

The leading figures in the Atlantic trade were merchants in the western ports. At the beginning of the century, Bristol and Glasgow were the leaders; by the 1780s they had been equalled in importance by Liverpool had also taken the lead in the sordid side of trade. mostly 'sea-island cotton' from the West Indies. Liverpool had also taken the lead in the sordid side of trade. Ships left for Africa where their captains exchanged cargoes for slaves held in pens by African slavers. They then carried them across the 'middle passage' of the Atlantic and auctioned them to planters in America or the Caribbean. The return journey on this triangular trade was made with cotton, sugar, tobacco or timber.

Trade with the east was different. To trade in India, the East Indies or China a merchant had to belong to the East India Company and use its trading posts for collecting tea, silk, drugs and spices, as well as porcelain and furniture. The value of these imports was not balanced by exports because India and China had their own textile, metal and porcelain manufactures.

Protectionism

Merchants had to obey a long list of regulations which were later lumped together as 'protectionism'. It was a European-wide system which each country used to protect its manufacturing against competition. Each state put customs duties on imports so that they cost more than the same items made at home, but other regulations went further. In Britain it was illegal to export raw wool which might help foreign cloth-makers or to import printed calicoes because they would rival cloth printed here. For the same reasons machinery could not be exported nor could skilled mechanics emigrate.

British merchants and ship-owners were protected by the seventeenth-century Navigation Acts. These made it illegal for a Dutch or French ship to collect goods from a British colony and take them to Holland or France or even to Britain. All colonial goods had to be carried in British-owned ships with mostly British crews. The Navigation Acts were backed up by preferential customs duties. If timber came in from a

A

A1 The direction of trade, 1784–6.

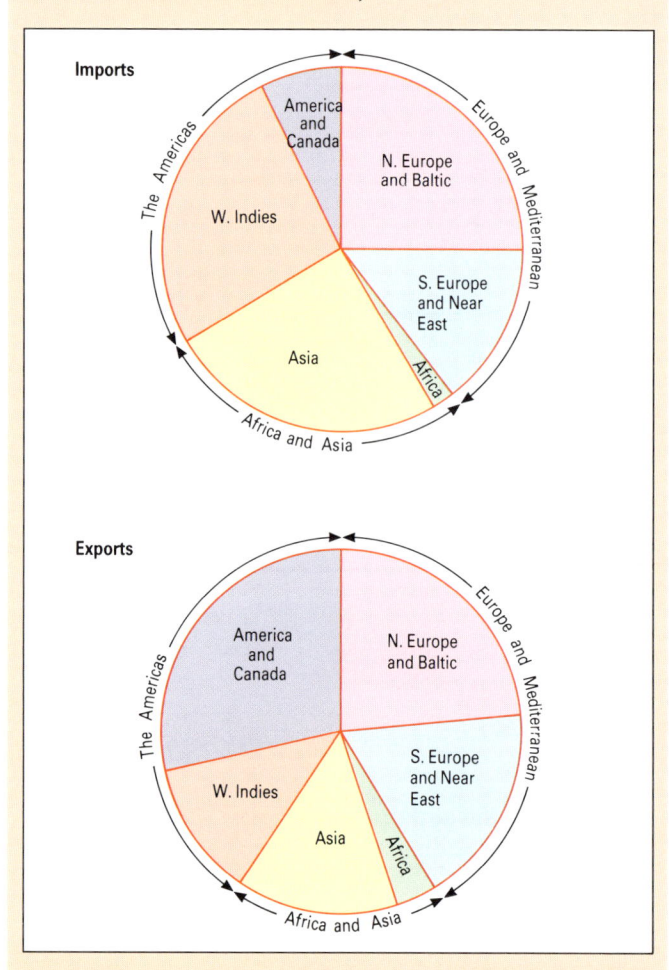

A2 Sales to Europeans in the West Indies.

...woollen, linen, silk, iron, brass, leather, glass, chinaware, clocks, watches, jewels, wrought plate, gold and silver, lace, medicines...gunpowder... bricks, paint, oil, cordage, sugar pots, drips, hoops, candles, pipes, swords, pistols, walking canes... grindstones, paving stones, books, toys, stationery, cutlery, Birmingham and haberdashery wares, all sorts of household goods and furniture, wearing apparel, cabinet ware, chariots, chaises, coppers ...in short all things necessary for life and almost the whole consumption is British manufacture.

John Campbell, *Candid and impartial considerations of the Nature of the Sugar Trade*, 1763

1. What connection can you see between the 1784–6 list of imports on page 11 and the information on the top chart.
2. Which items in source A2 were most likely to have come from a) London, b) the midlands, c) Sheffield, d) Bristol?
3. What does John Campbell mean by the last two lines?

foreign country such as Norway it paid a duty of 55%. If it came from a British colony such as Canada it paid only 10%. The Acts reserved work for British ship-owners, seamen and boat-builders and they created the re-export trade. Far more sugar, tobacco, tea and other goods came into Britain than could be sold here. Often as much as three-quarters came no further than a dock-side warehouse where the barrels or bundles waited for another ship to carry them to Europe.

Trade and industry

Overseas traders imported raw materials for textile workers, sugar refiners, tobacco curers and smaller trades such as making furniture with central American timber or hats from furs trapped in Canada. Just as important, they opened up new overseas markets. The main textile and iron districts got the biggest benefit but less well known places had their share. In 1700, Kendal had 2,000 people; by 1800 it had 8,000 working in tanning, hosiery and making gunpowder. Many of these products went overseas from London or Liverpool.

Sometimes merchants decided that the best way to keep a regular flow of goods going overseas was to become a manufacturer themselves. In other cases merchants lent money to manufacturers who were producing goods they could sell overseas.

Banking

A man buying a Newcomen steam engine for his mines might need £300; mules for a workshop came to about £30 each and if they were to be driven by water the work would cost about £200. Sometimes they paid out of their savings, but usually they borrowed and paid interest on the loan. Today lending and borrowing of this sort is everyday business for the branches of the main banks. At the beginning of the eighteenth century, most banks were in London. They had been started by people who could not avoid having wealth stored in their workplaces or warehouses. Many of the early ones were goldsmiths or silversmiths. They often called this stock of precious metal their 'bank'.

From having your own store or bank it was an easy step to storing other people's wealth and giving them notes saying that you promised to give the bearer so much gold or silver (which was known as sterling) when they handed it in. You could also lend money and the borrower would give you a note saying that he would give you a certain sum (which was what he borrowed plus interest) on a certain date, perhaps three, six or twelve months ahead. These promissory notes were the beginnings of the modern bank note. A man who had a promissory note from a bank for a hundred guineas could use it to buy goods from a merchant who would hand it in to the bank or use it himself to buy goods.

One London bank was special. The Bank of England had been started in 1694 to make loans to the government mostly to pay for wars. It specialised in issuing Exchequer Bills which said that the government would repay a certain sum on a certain date. These too could be passed around between people buying and selling goods.

After 1700, the London banking system began to be copied in other parts of the country. Men such as merchant clothiers or iron-mongers often had a long time to wait before the wool or iron rods they gave to hand-workers were made into goods which could be sold. They did not pay cash for these materials but gave a promissory note or bill of exchange saying they would pay in three or six months. Often these notes or bills passed through many hands. Some merchants went into banking as a sideline. They would cash these bills or notes for a little less than they were worth so they would make a profit to lend to someone else.

By about 1750, a dozen of these operators had set up the first country banks which was the term given for banks outside London. The number grew in the following years especially when some of the larger manufacturers set up banks. One was the iron-master, Sampson Lloyd, (whose slitting mills were described in Unit 1B) who joined with a button manufacturer to set up Taylor and Lloyd's bank in Birmingham in 1765.

B

A note issued in 1810 by one of the 600 private banks.

4. In which ways is this a) different from and b) similar to a modern bank note?

21

F SKILLS SECTION

Reading a writer of the time

Unit 1E should have helped you to understand how sources are used to build up a historical account. Students of history also need to be able to use their knowledge to help them understand writings from the time. All these extracts are taken from the writings of one man, Arthur Young. Between 1768 and 1810 he wrote many books and journals mostly about agriculture but they also included references to manufacturing and transport.

Make notes for each extract to show:
1. How it describes an aspect of handwork manufacturing (like those in Part One).
2. How it describes the result of new inventions, methods of working, technology, trade or transport.
3. Two page references from Part One or Part Two which give you background information which helps you to understand what Arthur Young is describing.

Warrington
...the manufacture of sail-cloth and sacking are very considerable. The first is spun by women and girls who earn about 2d a day. It is then bleached which is done by men, who earn 10s a week; after bleaching it is wound by women, whose earnings are 2s 6d a week...The last operation is the weaving in which the men earn 9s, the women 5s, and boys 3s 6d a week.

Northern Tour, 1771

Sheffield
In the cutlery branch there are several sub-divisions, such as razor, scissor, lancets, flems etc. Among these the grinders make the greatest earnings; 18s, 19s and 20s a week are common...the grindstones turn with such amazing velocity that by the mere force of motion they now and then fly in pieces and kill the men. Many grindstones are turned by a set of wheel which all receive their motion from one water-wheel...

Northern Tour, 1771

Newcastle
The coal waggon roads, from the pits to the water, are great works, carried over all sorts of inequalities of ground...The tracks of the wheels are marked with pieces of timber let into the road for the wheels to run on, by which means one horse is enabled to draw, and that with ease, fifty or sixty bushels of coal...

Northern Tour, 1771

Coalbrookdale
The waggon ways that lead down to the river, instead of wood, are laid with cast iron...Past his new slitting mills, which are not finished, but the immense wheels 20 feet in diameter of cast iron were there.

A Tour in Shropshire, 1776

Birmingham
The capital improvement wrought since I was here before is the canal to Oxford, Coventry, Wolverhampton, &c...I looked around me with amazement at the change effected in twelve years; so great that this place may now be probably reckoned, with justice, the first manufacturing town in the world. From these...quays you may now go by water to Hull, Liverpool, Bristol, Oxford (130 miles) and London.

Annals of Agriculture, 1791

Knowledge and understanding

Make a chart like this for the people listed below.

Name	One key fact	Significance
Matthew Boulton	Opened Soho Manufactory, 1763	Helped speed up move of handworkers from homes to workshops with machinery. Used water-power and latest means of transport.

Jeddediah Strutt
James Hargreaves
Richard Arkwright
Samuel Crompton
Abraham Darby I
Benjamin Huntsman
Thomas Newcomen
John Wilkinson
James Brindley
John Smeaton
Josiah Wedgwood

Before you read on:

With the help of page 11, remind yourself of the great changes that had taken place in the output of manufacturing, trade and transport by the 1780s, and how towns were growing as new inventions led to many workshops being opened. All this was done without the help of steam power. Part Three shows how steam power became important in some major industries.

3

1780s – 1850: FROM MANUFACTURING TO INDUSTRY

How textiles, iron engineering and coal-mining developed into mechanised large-scale industries.

- A Steam power
- B Cotton: the take-off
- C Textiles: the power revolution
- D Textiles: workers, unions and the law
- E Iron
- F Coal
- G Iron roads
- H Skills section: studying a picture source

Industry around 1851

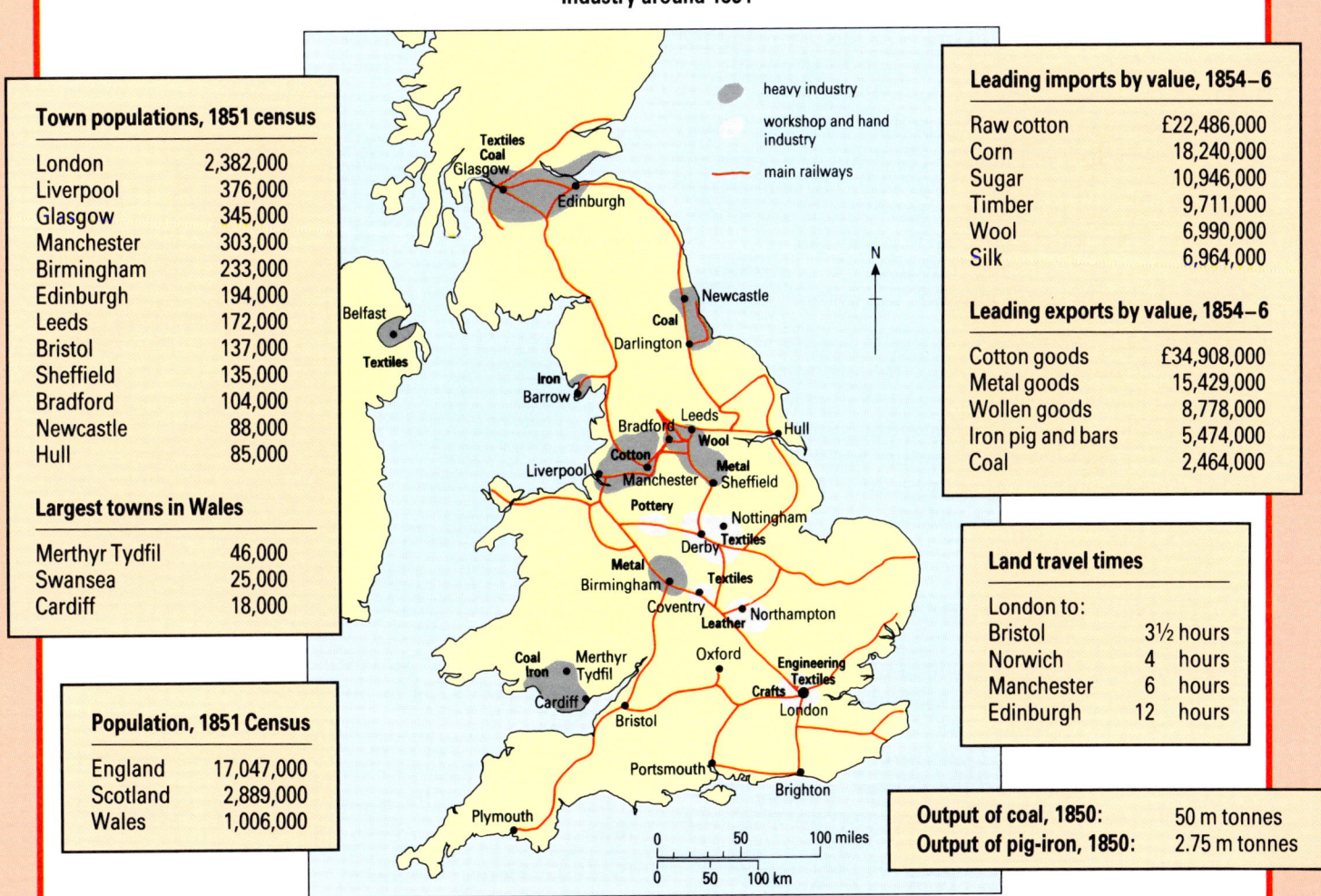

Town populations, 1851 census

London	2,382,000
Liverpool	376,000
Glasgow	345,000
Manchester	303,000
Birmingham	233,000
Edinburgh	194,000
Leeds	172,000
Bristol	137,000
Sheffield	135,000
Bradford	104,000
Newcastle	88,000
Hull	85,000

Largest towns in Wales

Merthyr Tydfil	46,000
Swansea	25,000
Cardiff	18,000

Population, 1851 Census

England	17,047,000
Scotland	2,889,000
Wales	1,006,000

Leading imports by value, 1854–6

Raw cotton	£22,486,000
Corn	18,240,000
Sugar	10,946,000
Timber	9,711,000
Wool	6,990,000
Silk	6,964,000

Leading exports by value, 1854–6

Cotton goods	£34,908,000
Metal goods	15,429,000
Wollen goods	8,778,000
Iron pig and bars	5,474,000
Coal	2,464,000

Land travel times

London to:
Bristol	3½ hours
Norwich	4 hours
Manchester	6 hours
Edinburgh	12 hours

Output of coal, 1850: 50 m tonnes
Output of pig-iron, 1850: 2.75 m tonnes

Before you read on:

a) Compare this information with that on page 11. How would you summarise the changes in town size, overseas trade, output of iron and coal and travel times.
b) What do the maps suggest about changes in the balance of population between different parts of the country?

A STEAM POWER

Boulton and Watt

James Watt was a skilled scientific instrument maker with a knowledge of physics (although he would call it natural philosophy) and what it said about subjects such as heat transfer. In 1764 he repaired a model of a Newcomen engine used in lectures in Glasgow University. He was struck by how it wasted heat which meant it was expensive on coal. Below the piston, the cylinder was cooled with water after every stroke. Above the piston, it was cooled by air entering the open top. Watt made an model which drew the steam from the cylinder to be cooled in a separate condenser and put a seal on top with a hole for the piston rod.

To make a full-sized version he went into partnership with John Roebuck, the man who started the Carron ironworks. They built an engine but could not make the cylinder and piston fit closely. Watt wanted to find another partner but Roebuck refused to let him. Then he went bankrupt in 1773 and sold his share in the engine to Matthew Boulton. He and Watt rebuilt the engine at the Soho Manufactory in Birmingham – still with the leaking cylinder. Boulton then asked his friend, the iron-master John Wilkinson, to make a new one on his cannon-boring machine (Unit 2D). He delivered it in April 1775 and the Boulton and Watt steam engine was born. They patented it so it could not legally be copied for twenty-five years. In that time they sold about 450 and Wilkinson made most of the cylinders.

The other parts were made in the Soho Manufactory and assembled on the spot under the eye of the firm's foreman, William Murdoch. He and Watt converted the engine to rotary action by adding the 'sun and planet' motion in 1781. It worked smoothly when they added parallel motion and a governor. Now a rotary engine could be used wherever a wheel turned by hand, horse or water had been used before.

Steam power and industry

In 1800 there were about 2,000 steam engines in Britain. About 800 were Newcomen engines for pumping. Most of the rotary engines went to ironworks to make the blast or to work hammers and rollers. In mines they wound miners and coal up the deepest shafts. Several were bought by flour mills. Textile factory-owners were slower to take up the steam engine.

As soon as the Boulton and Watt patent expired, new forms of the steam engine appeared. In 1802 Richard Trevithick made one using high pressure steam. It was also 'direct-acting' so that it did not need a beam to turn the wheel. In 1804 Trevithick put it on wheels to pull seventy men and ten tonnes of iron bars from Merthyr Tydfil to the canal nine miles away. In 1812 he built the first giant Cornish engine which used pressure at forty pounds per square inch compared with the five to ten pounds in a Watt engine. From then on Cornish engines were used for really heavy work such as pumping a town's water.

In 1807 Henry Maudslay, a machine-tool specialist, made his table-top high pressure engine which was ideal for engineering workshops. It was so precisely made that it was the origin of the engines used in steam boats. In 1845 John McNaught found a way of converting single engines into compound engines with two cylinders. They saved two-thirds of the fuel used by a Watt engine.

By the 1850s, steam had not completely triumphed except in most of the coal, iron and textile industries.

A

James Watt wrote to John Smeaton, who was engineering adviser to the Carron ironworks.

> Mr Wilkinson has improved the art of boring cylinders so that I promise upon a 72 inch cylinder being not further from absolute truth than the thickness of a thin sixpence in the worst part.

James Watt to John Smeaton, 1776

1. What improvement is James Watt describing? Why was it vital to the steam engine's success?
2. What thoughts might have gone through Smeaton's mind when he read this letter?

B

A Watt engine of 1788.

3. How simply can you explain the difference between this engine and Newcomen's engine on page 19?

C

Trevithick's engine, 1802.

4. Can you see evidence that the engine uses high pressure?
5. What is the difference between the way the wheels are driven in this engine and in Watts's engine?

D

The horse-power of steam engines in use in Britain:

1800	20,000 hp
1824	100,000 hp
1850	300,000 hp
1870	977,000 hp
1900	9,659,000 hp

6. Turn these figures into a graph. What does it tell you about steam power after 1850? Suggest reasons for the development you describe.

There were still far more people making clothes, hats, gloves or shoes in cottages and workshops than there were in steam-powered textile factories. Yet steam power was on its way to becoming the basis of industry. Already anyone building a new factory, brewery, newspaper printing-press or flour mill, would begin with steam.

By the 1850s, mechanical engineering had become an industry in its own right. The day of the millwright installing a water wheel or local craftsmen putting up a Newcomen or Watt engine had long gone. They had been replaced by engineering firms with specialist workers such as smiths, fitters, pattern makers, mechanics and boiler makers. Many of these new firms could be found in Manchester and Leeds because textile manufacturers, based in the north, were the biggest customers for power-driven machinery to use in their mills.

E

William Fairburn and Son's Manchester works, 1839. The steam-powered machine on the right punches holes in boiler plates.

7. List the objects or activities you can identify.
8. How might this be used as evidence for progress in a) the engineering and b) the iron industry?

B COTTON: THE TAKE-OFF

In the 1780s the cotton industry started a dramatic rise. Output went on to double every ten years until the 1850s. By then it was a mechanical industry in steam-powered factories. But there was a long 'take-off' for the journey to industrialisation. The workers in these take-off years could be found in either valley mill-communities or one of Lancashire's growing towns.

A

Some reasons for increased cotton output:

> Now cotton yarn is cheaper than linen yarn, and cotton goods are very much used in place of... expensive fabrics of flax; and they have almost totally superseded the silks. Women of all ranks from the highest to the lowest, are clothed in British manufactures of cotton... they stand the washing as well as to appear fresh and new every time they are washed.
>
> *Macpherson's Annals of Commerce*, 1785

1. How does the writer explain the boom in sales?
2. What reasons do you know for cotton replacing flax and linen?

The valley factory-masters

In the 1780s and 1790s Richard Arkwright was just one pioneer of a new kind of working community. Nearly all his mills were in valleys in Derbyshire, Lancashire and Scotland. The Strutt family built theirs in the Derbyshire valley town of Belper, and Samuel Greg opened his at Styal on the River Bollin, south of Manchester. Their mills used powerful water-wheels like those developed by John Smeaton (Unit 2D).

By 1781 Arkwright's two mills in Cromford had 1,000 workers and only one in twelve was an adult male, usually a mechanic, warehouseman or clerk. Mill-owners had difficulties in finding enough women and children. One solution was to open workshops with looms or knitting frames which would draw men to the area so their wives and children could work in the mill.

B

> Darley Cotton Mill. Wanted, Families, particularly women and children to work at the said mill. They may be provided with comfortable houses and every necessary convenience... particularly a milking cow to each family. It is a very good neighbourhood for the men getting work who are not employed in the manufactory.

3. Apart from housing what other incentive is offered to workers?

Many masters were proud of the social benefits they offered. The Strutts built Sunday schools for their young workers to attend (on their only free day). Several owners built chapels or churches and market-halls as well as houses. The other side of the coin was the way the masters set out to turn workers into an obedient factory labour-force. Mills had bells to signal the start of the day which was usually thirteen hours including one for lunch, Monday to Saturday. There were fines for lateness, carelessness and for trivial offences, such as calling through windows. Very often the workers who had these fines docked from their wages were seven or eight years old. 'Overlookers' beat child workers.

Several mill-owners made up for the shortage of workers by using 'apprentices' supplied by poor law officers. Robert Owen wrote about how his father-in-law, David Dale, treated 'apprentices' from workhouses in Edinburgh at New Lanark in Scotland:

C

> These children were to be fed, clothed and educated; and these duties Mr. Dale performed with unwearied benevolence... The rooms provided were spacious, always clean and well-ventilated; the food was abundant... But to defray the expenses... it was absolutely necessary that the children should be employed within the mills from six o'clock in the morning till seven in the evening, summer and winter and after these hours their education commenced.
>
> It is not to be supposed that children so young could remain... in constant employment on their feet within cotton mills and, afterwards acquire much proficiency in education... many of them became dwarfs in mind and body...
>
> Robert Owen, *A New View of Society*, 1831

4. What evidence is there that David Dale was a good employer by the standards of his time?
5. What was Robert Owen's view of his father-in-law's treatment of apprentices?

In 1795 Robert Owen took charge of the New Lanark mills after he had married David Dale's daughter. He refused to employ any child under ten. Before that they had to spend five years in a company school which Owen called the Institution for the Formation of Character. When children went to work they found a wooden block hanging over each of their places. This was Owen's 'silent monitor'. Each day the overseer turned it to one of its four coloured sides to show how he graded the worker's work and behaviour. Outsiders admired the monitor but there is no evidence about how workers felt about it or whether parents would have preferred children to work and earn as they had almost certainly done themselves at six or seven.

D

A painting of New Lanark published in 1825.

6. What impression does the painter give of New Lanark as a place to live and work?

Lancashire towns

The Lancashire towns had many more people than the valley communities but the first textile factories meant something very different. Most of the spinning machines were mules which were smaller than Arkwright's frame and a local historian described how they were:

E

> ...erected in garrets or lofts, and many a dilapidated barn and cowshed was patched up in the walls, repaired in the roof and provided with windows, to serve as a lodging room for the new muslin wheels.
>
> R. Guest, *A Compendious History of the Cotton Manufacture*, 1823

7. How would the owner of this sort of workshop be different from an Arkwright or a Strutt?

In 1821 Manchester had sixty-six spinning mills. A few were large enough to compare with Arkwright's but on average they had only ninety workers each and two-thirds of them were in shared buildings. Steam power came slowly. Many manufacturers decided it was too expensive to convert from water power until the 1820s.

F

A cotton town, Bolton in 1793 and 1824.

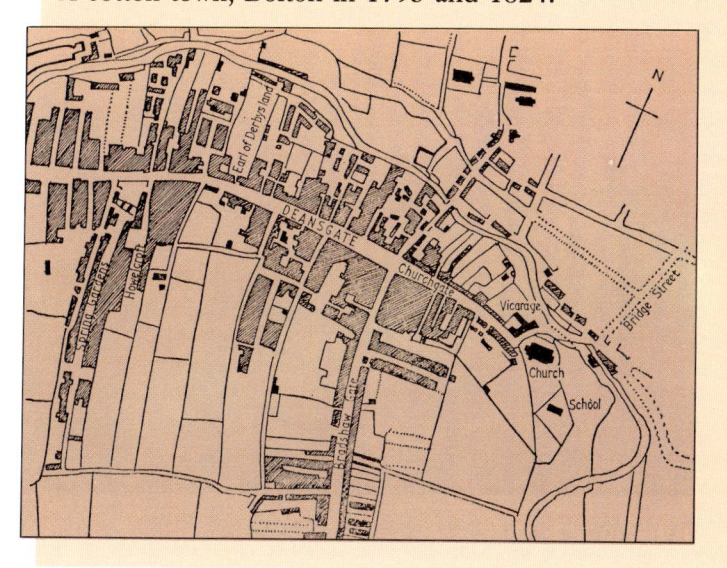

Early mules needed strength because a wheel had to be turned to twist the yarn while water or steam turned the spindles. This put the job into the hands of men. Mules needed piecers and scavengers and spinners took their own or neighbours' children as assistants. There were few women Mule workers because up to the 1820s many women still worked in jenny workshops.

The handloom weavers

Up to the 1810s and into the 1820s so much yarn was produced on jennies, mules and frames that there was work for many more handloom weavers than before the inventions. Stories were told about weavers showing off their wealth by wearing five-pound notes in their hats. If any really did this it would be the skilled men who could weave the finest and most expensive cotton in workshops. It was a different matter for the man weaving plain and cheap cloth. The skill could be learned in a few weeks and it was taken up by tens of thousands of cottage workers in nearby villages and also by poorer men who moved from agricultural labouring to work in the towns. Their looms were often in damp cellars, their piece rates were low and they had give up earning time to taking in their cloth and collecting more yarn.

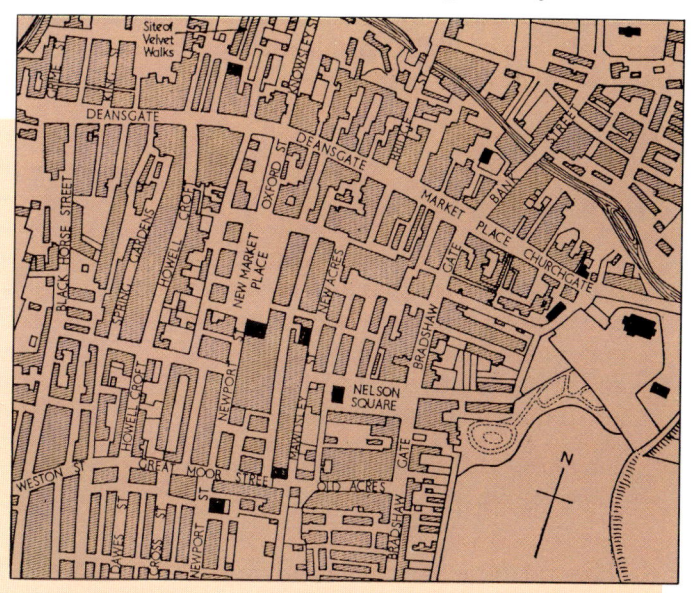

8. List the main developments between the maps.
9. What difference does this suggest between life and work in a valley community like New Lanark and a mill town like Bolton?

C TEXTILES: THE POWER REVOLUTION

Cotton manufacturers were slower than owners of mines and ironworks to introduce steam power. When they did they were likely to choose an engine made by a local firm which knew the textile industry and could install new machinery at the same time. In Leeds there was the firm of Matthew Murray who began as a textile machine-maker and concentrated on compact engines for use in small mills. In Lancashire there was Peel & Williams and Bateman & Sharratt (or Sharrard).

Sales from such firms to cotton manufacturers were slow until the 1810s. Often the thing which made them change over was the coming of power looms. The first one had been made by a clergyman, Edmund Cartwright, in 1783 but it was clumsy and often broke down. By around 1810 power looms were much more efficient and some manufacturers built a power weaving-shed onto their spinning mill. The workers were nearly all women. Many of them could no longer find work as jenny spinners because as mules became larger and more powerful the jenny workshops were forced to close down.

In the 1830s new mules were 'self-acting' which meant that both the spinning and twisting was done by steam power. Men still held on to the job but now they would need up to eight or nine children or young women assistants. The factory-owner, not the mule spinner, now chose them and put them in the charge of overlookers. New mills were built, solid many-storeyed buildings with huge floors taken up by rows of mules, looms or carding machines. Many of them still tower over houses in Lancashire towns to this day.

The 1851 census showed that three-quarters of cotton workers were in factories and seven-eighths of the factories were driven by steam. It also showed that there were only about 50,000 handloom weavers compared with five times that number in the 1820s. Steam power had nearly destroyed the trade altogether and often those who were left could only work when mill-owners had a bigger order than their machines could cope with.

The geography of textiles

Cotton was the first product to complete the change from eighteenth-century manufacturing to nineteenth-century industry. By 1851, a woollen industry was developing in Yorkshire but it was by no means complete. Around Bradford, worsteds were made out of the longer wool fibres which were easy to spin and weave by machine. So spinning and weaving moved over to steam in the 1820s and 1830s just as in Lancashire. The main districts for woollens, which use shorter threads, were around Leeds and Huddersfield. Spinning became a power-based town industry in the 1820s but power weaving was slower to develop. In 1850 there were still as many hand weavers as power weavers.

The Lancashire and Yorkshire textile industries were leading one of the great changes in nineteenth-century geography. Eighteenth-century manufacturing had often been spread across many districts. Woollen cloths of different kinds were made in parts of Scotland and Wales, in East Anglia around Norwich and in the south-west of England. By 1851 Lancashire made more than 90% of all the cotton (and most of the rest was produced around the River Clyde in Scotland). Yorkshire towns made about three-quarters of the woollen goods, and already the industry had died out in Norwich and some other centres. A few manufacturers managed to survive in the West Country by building steam-powered factories to make some of the finer cloths. There was a small carpet-making industry around Kidderminster and blanket-making workshops were often opened near railway stations in Wales. Yet even their products had to

A

A1 Bateman & Sharrard, 1795.

> ...Mr Sharrard is a very ingenious and able engineer, who has improved upon and brought the steam engine to great perfection. Most of those that are used and set up in and about Manchester are of their make and fitting up...

John Aikin, *A Description of the Country from Thirty to Forty Miles round Manchester*, 1795

1. How do these sources help to explain why the Lancashire towns became the leading centres of the cotton industry, rather than the valley mill sites?
2. What means of transport can be seen in the picture?

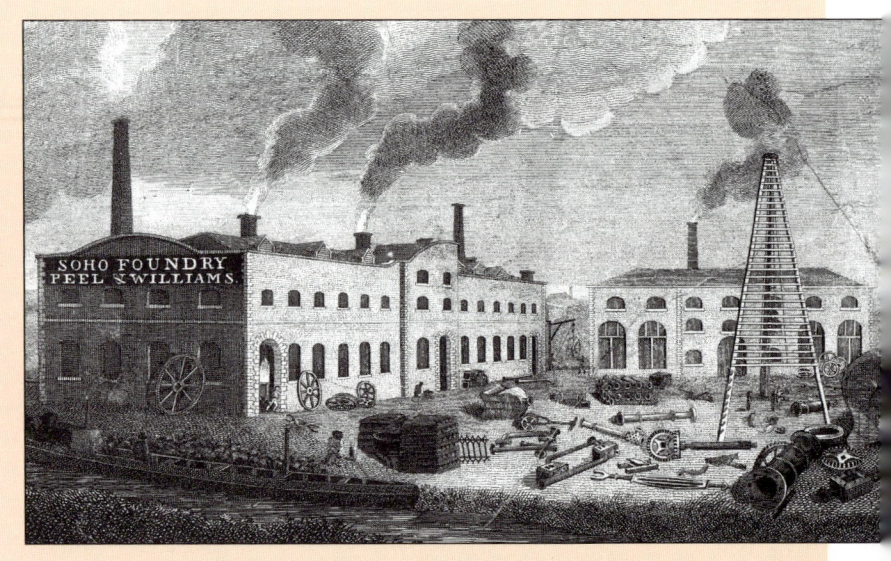

A2 Peel & Williams works in Manchester, 1814.

B

A cotton mill on fire, 1802.

3. What does this suggest about a common hazard of early industrial work?

C

Printing calico for dress-making, 1834.

4. Why was it worthwhile for cotton manufacturers to pay for such expensive machinery?

compete with the growth of specialisms in Yorkshire where towns became centres for carpets, blankets, felt or shoddy (made from shredded old cloth) as well as the different qualities of worsted and woollen cloth.

The Lancashire and Yorkshire towns dominated the industry because they were far more than bases for spinning and weaving. Many became important centres for machinery making. Very often there were coal-mines in or near the towns. Many other trades grew around cloth-making. Two important examples were printing and bleaching.

One in eight textile workers had a job in dying or bleaching. Once, bleaching had been done by wetting cloth with sour milk and stretching it out on 'tenterhooks' to whiten naturally. By the 1830s it was often done in steam-driven spinners using bleaching powder which was also made in the many chemicals works in Lancashire and Yorkshire.

D

Bleaching, formerly a process occupying weeks, might now be almost completed in the process of twenty-four hours, so that calicos which a Manchester manufacturer dispatches to his bleacher on the outskirt of the town early on one day, he *might* receive on the next... be conveyed on the same night (as is by no means uncommon) along the railway to the docks at Liverpool, and by a rapid shipment be on their voyage to a distant country within little more than forty-eight hours.

J. Wheeler, *Manchester, Its Political, Social and Commercial History*, 1836

5. In which ways does this account help to explain why the large towns became centres of industry?

D TEXTILES: WORKERS, UNIONS AND THE LAW

The workers change their views

In 1819 Sir Robert Peel MP put a Factory Act to Parliament. He was a mill-owner himself, the son of the man who had encouraged James Hargreaves (Unit 2A). His Act had the backing of Robert Owen and said that no child of nine years or under could work in a textile factory. Between ten and sixteen their hours should be limited to twelve a day. Employers simply ignored the Act and there were no factory inspectors to see that it was obeyed. But workers also ignored it. It seemed natural enough for their children to work, and at that time most children were either in a jenny workshop with their mother or a mule-spinning factory with their father.

Ten years or so later, opinion among workers was changing. One reason was that there were much larger mules in larger factories and one mule operator needed up to nine assistants who were both children and young women. Now employers chose the young workers and they were put under the charge of overseers not parents or relatives. There were also many more mule factories and more men mule-spinners who began to try to band together to protect their jobs and their wages. They had several grievances. When trade was bad, employers closed the mills or put the workers on short time – and short pay. They accused the masters of trying to replace them with cheaper female labour. In 1829 Lancashire spinners struck for fourteen weeks against reduced wages. The strike failed but it led to one of the first trade unions, the Cotton Operatives Union led by John Doherty. It lasted only a short time but its members were soon active in the Short Hours Movement which spread rapidly in the 1830s.

The Short Hours Movement

Apart from the mill-workers, many other people criticised the factory-owners. Some of the criticism came from political rivalry. Mill-owners were usually Whig, so their enemies were usually Tory. Tories were often landowners with a dislike for the new industrialists. They could find support from clergymen who believed that factory work and town life was bad for morals. Some doctors who had first-hand experience of town conditions also joined the anti-factory side. There were even some Tory mill-owners such as John Fielden whose mills were in the Yorkshire hills – away from the filth and harsh conditions in the towns. In Parliament the main enemy of the mill-owners was the social reformer, Lord Shaftesbury.

These people thought that the greatest evil of factories was the hours worked by children. In 1832 the campaign had grown so strong that the government set up a Royal Commission to hear evidence.

The Royal Commission led to the 1833 Factory Act which was a compromise which tried to suit both sides. The law was full of holes. It was easy to lie about the age of a child worker and there could be no proof of being nine years old until nine years after the first birth certificates were issued in 1837. No standards were laid down for schools. In at least one mill, the 'teacher' was the illiterate boiler man. Worst of all, mill-owners simply worked the children in relays and kept factories open for up to fifteen hours. The campaign against children's labour went on.

A

Arguments before the Royal Commission.

A1

After the children from eight to twelve years had worked eight or nine hours or ten hours, they were nearly ready to faint; some were asleep; some were only kept to work by being spoken to, or by a little chastisement, to make them jump up. I was sometimes obliged to chastise them when they were almost fainting, and it hurt my feelings; then they would spring up and work pretty well for another hour; but the last two or three hours were my hardest work, for they then got so exhausted.

A2

Hand-loom weavers, frame work knitters, lace runners and work people engaged in other lines of domestic manufacture are in most cases worked at an earlier age for longer hours and for less wages than the body of children employed in factories.

Royal Commission on Factory Employment, 1832

1. What was the likely occupation of the man giving the first piece of evidence?
2. What is the point being made by the second witness?

B

The 1833 Factory Act.
- Children under nine could not work and children aged nine to thirteen could work only eight hours per day. They could only do this if they also spent two hours in a factory school.
- Young persons between thirteen and eighteen could work only twelve hours a day.
- There were to be factory inspectors to see that the law was obeyed.

3. Compare this law with the 1819 Factory Act. Which differences would please a) the employers and b) the campaigners?

C

Propaganda techniques: nineteenth-century style.

C1 is from *The History of Cotton Manufacture*, written in 1835 by Edward Baines who was an admirer of the changes that were taking place. C2 is an illustration in a novel, *The Life and Adventures of Michael Armstrong, Factory Boy*, written in 1840 by Francis Trollope a supporter of the campaign against children's work. It first appeared in black and white; colours were added later. Both show a man mule-spinner turning a wheel to move the carriage which held a row of spindles, a young woman piecer twisting broken ends together and a child scavenger picking up waste.

C1

C2

4. Where did the 1840 illustrator get his setting for the picture?
5. In which ways has he changed the scene? Why do you think he did this?
6. Which picture is likely to be the most truthful?

When the Short Hours Movement realised that the 1833 Act was not leading to real improvements, they began to press for shorter hours for women to make it more difficult for owners to keep the factories running for so long. Their strongest point was that factory work made women less able to be good wives and mothers. Lord Shaftesbury put it this way when he quoted a factory inspector's summary of a mill workers' day:

D

Half an hour to dress and suckle her infant and carry it out to nurse; one hour for household duties before leaving home; half an hour for actually travelling to the mill; twelve hours actual labour; one and a half hours for meals; half an hour for returning home at night; one and a half hours for household duties and preparing for bed, leaving six and a half hours for recreation, seeing and visiting friends and sleep.

Hansard, 1844

Shaftesbury got the support of MPs for the 1844 Act – but it was another compromise:

> The starting age was cut to eight but children from eight to thirteen could work only 6½ hours. Women and young persons (13–18) could work for only twelve hours.

In 1847 the Ten Hours Act came at last. Now women and young persons could not work longer than ten hours. At first this was hailed as a great triumph and women certainly benefitted as one told a factory inspector:

E

I get 10s with ten hours; and would get 12s with twelve hours. I prefer ten hours. I have my family and house to look after, and I can go to bed sooner than I used to. I have sometimes been up twenty hours out of the twenty-four.

Report by Leonard Horner, 1849

7. Compare this with the inspector's statement in D. What would be the change in the number of hours the second woman spent out of the home?

Yet the Act said that the ten hours could be worked between 5.30am and 8.30pm so factory-owners could still have women work in relays and keep men at a standard 13½ hour day. That was ended in 1850 with a law which said that the working day should be 6am to 6pm with 1½ hours for meals and no work after 2pm on Saturday. Today it would seem harsh to have a primary-school child work a 6½ hour day or even someone studying GCSE work for ten hours. Yet by 1850 textile factory-workers were better off than any others. They were the only group, apart from mine workers, with any laws to control their hours or their safety.

E IRON

Iron-working was the first 'heavy industry'. After the 1780s, cast-iron was important but many new products were made from wrought-iron – which first had to come out of the blast furnace as pig-iron.

Making the pig

The first leap in pig-iron output came when coke was used and furnaces could be larger. The next began in 1776 when John Wilkinson bought the second Boulton and Watt engine to replace the water-wheel which worked the blowing cylinder at one of his blast furnaces. Steam engines were soon in use in all large ironworks for blowing and for working hoists which lifted trucks of iron-ore and coke to the top of the new large furnaces.

A rule followed by all iron-masters was to keep the blast as cold as possible. In 1829 the manager of a Glasgow gas-works, J.B. Neilson, showed that better results came from heating the air and blowing in a hot blast:

A

During the first six months of the year 1833, one ton of cast-iron was made with 2 tons 5¼ cwt of raw coal – add to this 8 cwt of coal for heating. We have 2 tons 13¼ cwt of coal required to make a ton of iron, whereas in 1829, when the cold blast was in operation, 8 tons 1¼ cwt of coal was used.

H. Scrivenor, *History of the Iron Trade*, 1854

1. Roughly what fraction of coal was saved?

In 1832 a Black Countryman, John Gibbons, upset another old belief that the furnace hearth must be square. He tried a round one and it turned out 100 tonnes a week compared with 75 in a square hearth. A hundred tonnes was more than a furnace of the 1730s made in a year. By the 1850s up to 300 tonnes a week were common.

Working the wrought

Up to the 1770s pig-iron was reheated and hammered at a forge. In 1783 and 1784 the process was changed to an industrial one by Henry Cort at his forge in Hampshire. To reheat the pig-iron, he used a reverbatory furnace, divided into two by a bridge of firebricks. Coal burned on one side of the bridge and the flames bounced (or reverberated) down on to pig-iron in the other half. Carbon in the iron combined with oxygen and escaped as carbon monoxide. To help this take place the iron was stirred, or puddled, with an iron bar.

In the 1820s Joseph Hall, a Black Countryman, threw some waste slag into the puddling furnace. It was rich in iron oxide which combined with the carbon so that the iron began to boil. Pig boiling used only about half of the coal of Henry Cort's system. It also created one of the toughest jobs in industry. Each furnace was minded for a twelve-hour shift by a puddler and his assistant. During the half-hour boil, the two men took turns to stir four hundredweight of metal. Then they lifted it out in four huge balls which went straight to the steam hammers and then, still hot, to Cort's second invention, the rolling mill.

The mills were not new but Henry Cort's idea was. He cut grooves into the rollers so that they made rectangular bars. By around 1815 'three high rollers' had been invented so the iron could be rolled forward through the lower set and back through the upper.

Integration

In the days of water power, the furnace and forge had to be apart to avoid stealing each other's water. Steam

B

A rolling mill at the Cyfartha Works, with puddling furnaces on the right.

2. In which ways could this help to explain why Cyfartha produced more iron than any other works in the world at the time?
3. What evidence can you see of a use for rolled iron?

Nasmyth's own painting of his steam hammer.

power drew them together into integrated works. By the 1820s it was common to find works with one or two blast furnaces, a dozen puddling furnaces and several hammering forges and rolling mills. Often the works also owned its own coal-mines.

From the 1820s the rolling mills turned out hundreds of miles of railway track. There was a huge demand for wrought-iron plates to make locomotives and boilers for high-pressure steam engines, as well as girders for bridge building and thousands of tonnes of bars and rods which could be beaten into chains and tools. There were also new cast-iron products such as iron pipes for water and gas supplies.

An important sister industry was engineering. Ironworks often had a foundry where engine parts were cast for sale to specialist engineering firms. One in Manchester was owned by a Scot, James Nasmyth. He made half a dozen new machine-tools but his greatest invention was the steam hammer which could stamp an engine part from massive blocks of metal.

The iron districts

The integrated iron industry could survive only on large coalfields. Older centres such as Shropshire declined and by 1830 the industry was settled in three areas: the Black Country, South Wales and Clydeside in Scotland with smaller ones in Yorkshire and Derbyshire.

In 1788 the part of Staffordshire north-west of Birmingham had six coke furnaces. By 1850 there were nearly 160 in fifty integrated ironworks. There were seventeen towns with more than 10,000 people and it was difficult to see where one ended and another began. The area was already widely known as the Black Country. Queen Victoria is said to have ordered the carriage blinds to be pulled down as her train passed.

She had good reason. Everywhere you looked were mines, ironworks and waste heaps with rows of houses filling the spaces. The air was black with the smoke and grit, and foul with fumes from the countless piles of coal being slowly cooked into coke.

Jobs such as making screws and needles were being mechanised and were more likely to be in Birmingham or one of the larger towns. What was left was the heavy and the unskilled work. One example was the chain-making workshops where men hammered and joined thick rods into heavy chains while women worked on the lighter links. The poorly-paid work of nailing was often done by women as men nailers earned better money in the ironworks.

The Merthyr Tydfil ironworks were too far from centres of industry to sell a wide variety of iron goods. They specialised in products which could be made in bulk, especially wrought-iron bars and railway lines. The starting point for the growth of this industry was in 1786 when Richard Crawshay took over the Cyfartha Works and brought in Henry Cort's puddling and rolling. His three main rivals copied this and by 1850 the town was dominated by four huge integrated works (Cyfartha, Dowlais, Penydarren and Plymouth) with forty-seven blast furnaces between them and a work force of nearly 18,000. The town's population had grown from 8,000 in 1801 to 46,000 in 1851.

Eighteenth-century Scottish iron-making was based on water power at places such as the Carron works near Edinburgh. In 1801 the iron-master, David Mushet, discovered rich seams of blackband ore further west, near Glasgow. The ore got its name because it was streaked with coal. It was expensive to smelt until Neilson's hot-blast was used in 1829. Costs fell and Scottish iron production shot ahead. By 1850 the Clydeside ironworks were producing more than a quarter of all the iron made in Britain.

F COAL

In 1750 miners produced about 5 million tonnes of coal. A hundred years later output was 50 million. Without this huge increase there would have been no change from manufacturing to industry. Coal was vital for steam power and for the iron industry which used a quarter of all the coal mined in 1850.

New technology

The spearhead of this great change were the hewers who cut the coal from the seams. Up to the 1850s there were only the simplest improvements in their equipment. Iron picks and shovels replaced wood in the mid-eighteenth century. About then, too, many mines (except in the north-east) gave up the pillar and stall system where each hewer worked in a stall separated from the next by a pillar of coal. Instead all the coal along the seam was cut in the 'longwall' system and wooden pitprops were used to shore up the roofs of the roads and passages which led to the shaft.

Hewers were paid by the amount they sent to the surface. Most paid their own gang of women and children to be hauliers or drawers. These were words for lugging baskets or 'corves' of coal to the shaft. As mines grew larger, managers looked for ways to speed this up. They put trolleys in the main roads of the mines and drawers only had to haul the coal as far as them. In some mines, iron plateways were laid to run the trolleys on. Ponies were used wherever the roof was high enough. In many mines, these changes meant that fewer women could work. Drawing in the narrow passage-ways behind the hewer needed smaller bodies, often of children of around eight to ten. Hauling or leading ponies on the main roadway was work for teenage boys who would go on to be hewers at eighteen or nineteen. Yet there were still 5–6,000 women hauliers in 1841, many in Scotland.

It was only behind the hewer and the hauliers that steam power was used. By the 1750s a mine with a flooding problem could stay open by using a Newcomen engine to drain it. From the 1780s mine-owners could buy rotary engines to use at the top of the shaft instead of horse-whims. The extra power meant that men and coal could be hauled from much greater depths. From the 1820s some mines used underground winding engines to haul trolleys along the main passages using a new product of the iron industry, wire rope.

Steam and iron affected the position of mines. Up to the 1750s they were always near to the sea, a river or a canal. Then iron plateways and, later, rails were laid so horses could pull coal over a longer distance. In the early 1800s some mines used steam locomotives on these tracks. In the 1840s a network of public railways began to spread. Sending a tonne of coal by rail was only a quarter of the cost of sending it by canal.

The human cost

Mines were hot, dark, infested with rats, and foul smelling because there was no sanitation. Coal seams were often less than 45 cm high. Most miners who lived to middle age had ruptures and rheumatism. As to their lungs:

B

There are few young men above the age of twenty-five who are quite free from pectoral [chest] disease in some shape or other...Above the age of forty almost ALL miners are the subjects of chronic bronchitis and asthma...Ultimately his lungs are loaded with black matter, solid or fluid, like printers' ink or charcoal.

Miner and Workman's Advocate, 19 September 1863

A

A Northumberland pit, sketched in 1839.

1. Which uses of steam power can you identify?
2. What evidence is there of the iron industry's importance to mining?
3. How is the coal truck moved?

Between 1868 and 1919 one miner was killed every six hours, seriously crippled every two hours and injured enough to need a week off work every two minutes. There are no figures for before 1868 but they were probably worse. Accidents were caused by rock falls, being hit by a trolley, whiplashed with iron wire or by burns and scalds. Such things caused far more deaths than the disasters which killed a hundred or more.

A disaster usually meant an explosion which left miners trapped to die of suffocation. The main cause was fire-damp, or methane gas. A miner could ignite this with his candle and the blast would force its way through the narrow passage. To clear the methane, the pit had to be ventilated by having two shafts. A furnace was lit at the bottom of the upcast shaft to send the stale air up as if it was a chimney. If there was gas in this air you had an explosion and blocked shaft.

In 1810, John Buddle, a manager in a Northumberland colliery, worked out a system of air splitting. He used trapdoors to create separate currents with the bad air going out clear of the furnace. Young children were needed as trappers to open and close the doors as trolleys passed through. In 1841 there were about 5,000 boys and girls aged between five and ten doing this lonely job in the dark for nine or ten hours.

In 1812 an explosion trapped ninety-two men and boys at the Felling Colliery in Northumberland. A local committee asked the scientist, Humphrey Davy, to design a safer light. He made an oil lamp covered with a wire gauze which let in air but stopped the flame escaping. Some miners preferred the Geordie lamp made by George Stephenson which worked in the same way.

C

In 1830 John Buddle gave evidence to an enquiry about the value and dangers of safety lamps:

C1

Many collieries are now in existence, and old collieries have been re-opened, producing the best coals, which must have lain dormant but for the invention of the safety lamp.

C2

Scarcely a month occurs without the punishment of some of them for the mismanagement of the Davy lamps; they have been fined, and the magistrates have sent them to the house of correction for a month, yet they will screw off the top of the Davy, and expose the naked flame.

Evidence to House of Lords Select Committee on the Mines, 1830

4. How does the first extract explain the value of the safety lamp from the mine-owner's point of view?
5. Historians of mining believe that the safety lamp actually led to more explosions. What evidence does Buddle give which might support them?

The Mines Act

MPs showed more concern for women and children in factories than in mines until 1840 when Lord Shaftesbury called on them to set up a Commission to enquire into children's work in the mines. They agreed and twenty sub-commissioners were sent out to collect evidence. In 1842 they published their Report which dealt with women as well. The Report's illustrations and interviews were meant to grab readers' attention.

D

Betty Harris, a drawer. I have a belt round my waist, and a chain passing between my legs and I go on my hands and feet. The road is steep, and we have to hold by a rope... The pit is very wet where I work... I am not so strong as I was, and cannot stand my work so well as I used to do... the belt and chain is worse when we are in the family way.

Children's Employment Commission Report, 1842

6. Does this account help to explain why the first clause of the 1842 Mines Act said that no female should work underground?

The Report did the job Shaftesbury hoped for. MPs agreed that no females should work underground. Outside Parliament, many women miners protested that this would stop them doing the only kind of work open to them. MPs had a much hotter debate about the age boys could start underground. Shaftesbury wanted it to be twelve but supporters of the mine-owners forced this down to ten. The 1842 Act said one thing about safety. No boy under fifteen could be in charge of the engine letting miners up and down the shaft.

E

An illustration from the Commission's Report.

7. What part of a mine does this show?
8. Which two jobs are illustrated? Would they be the worst in the mine?
9. How would you know this is a nineteenth not eighteenth-century pit?
10. What form of lighting can you see? Would it be safe a) usually or b) always?

G IRON ROADS

The four ironworks opened at Merthyr Tydfil in the 1760s were forty miles up the Taff Valley from Cardiff. The only way to take iron to the sea was by pack-mule. The journey was slow and expensive because so many mules and drivers were needed. In winter it was often impossible because of the state of the track. The first step in tackling this came in 1771 when the Merthyr iron-masters played a leading part in setting up a turn-pike trust to build a firm road. After that, two tons of iron could be moved in a waggon drawn by four horses. In the 1780s the ironworks made about 10,000 tons a year.

In 1790 the iron-masters joined forces again, this time to form the Glamorganshire Canal Company to build a canal from Cardiff to Methyr. It was finished in 1794 and described in a guide book to Cardiff in 1818:

A

There are not less than 100,000 tonnes wrought iron of best manufacture shipped anually for London, and other places; the bulk of which is made at Merthyr Tydfil, and brought down from there by a curious navigable canal...the canal... is brought through a mountainous country with a wonderful ingenuity.

1. How had iron output increased in thirty years?
2. What ingenuity took canals through mountains?

The ingenuity was used to build fifty-one locks in twenty-five miles but locks slow barges down and the canal was greatly congested. In 1800 the masters of the three ironworks on the east of the valley decided to cut out the most congested part with a tramway from the Penydarren works into the canal 9½ miles further south. Iron rails were set on stone blocks and the tramway was open in 1802. One horse could now pull five carts or trams, each with a two-tonne load.

In 1804 Richard Trevithick was the first man to mount a steam engine on to a set of wheels. He used the high pressure engine he had invented the year before (source C Unit 3A) to haul wagons with ten tonnes of iron and seventy people from Penydarren Works to the Canal. The 9½ miles took him just over four hours but it was the first locomotive journey in history. It was repeated a few times but then given up because of the damage the locomotive did to the rails.

Many other coal and iron districts had used the same three solutions to their transport problems: turnpikes, canals and tramways. Tramways had become so common that one reason for the rapid growth of the iron industry was the rails that it turned out each year. The most complicated and lengthy web of tramways was in the coalfields around the Rivers Tyne and Tees. It was here that attempts were made to develop the fourth Merthyr Tydfil solution – steam locomotives instead of horses.

B

The canal and tramroad in the Taff Valley.

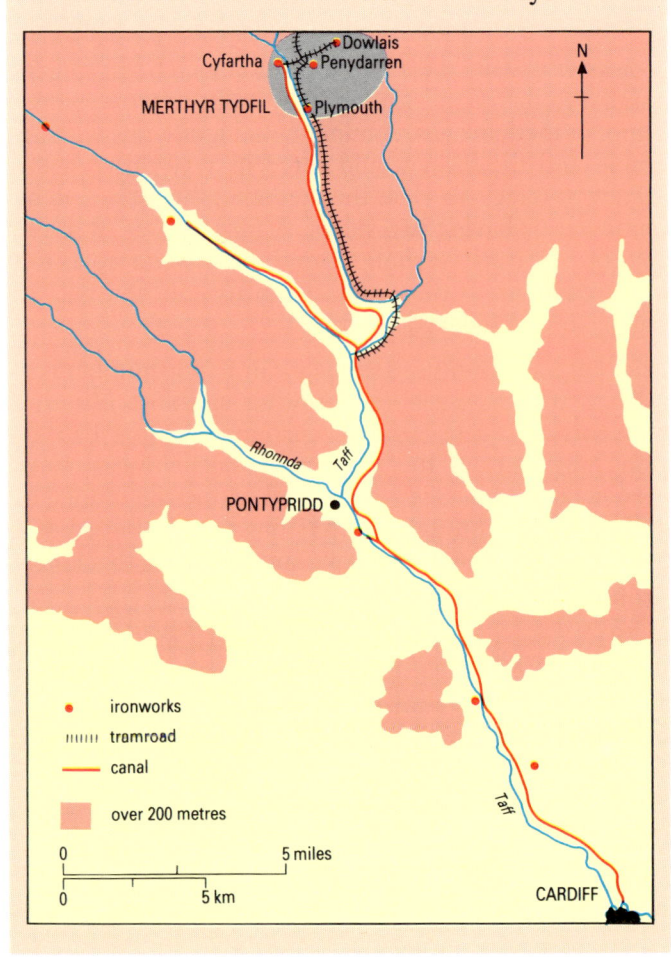

Map showing Merthyr Tydfil area (Cyfartha, Dowlais, Penydarren, Plymouth ironworks), Pontypridd, and Cardiff, with the Rhondda and Taff rivers. Legend: ironworks, tramroad, canal, over 200 metres. Scale: 5 miles / 5 km.

Copies of Trevithick's engines were made and found to break up the tracks just as they had at Penydarren. That was until George Stephenson, who was engineer to a group of mines, designed rails which fitted together snugly. In 1814 he built his first locomotive, *Blucher*, followed by a dozen more until he and his son Robert set up a locomotive-building firm in 1823. By then he was working for a company set up by businessmen in Stockton and Darlington who wanted to improve the transport of coal to their towns from mines to the west.

They had first thought of a canal but changed to a tramway. Stephenson persuaded them that they meant a 'Rail Way' for locomotives not a waggonway for horses. They agreed and he went on to build the 25½ miles of track using I-shaped wrought iron rails which had just become possible after an improvement to Cort's rolling process. Robert Stephenson & Co built a new engine, *Locomotion*, to run on about 20 miles of it. The rest of the distance was between two slopes where trucks would be wound up by wires on fixed steam engines. Horses were used to pull trucks between the slopes. This was the Stockton & Darlington Railway.

In many ways the Stockton & Darlington was the last of the tramways. For several years horses were used on the main track as often as locomotives. Yet it was also the first time that a public railway had been built where a canal would have been dug a few years earlier. Even before it was finished, Stephenson was planning a line between Liverpool and Manchester for a group of manufacturers and merchants who wanted to speed up freight between the two. They held the famous Rainhill locomotive trials in 1829 and George and Robert Stephenson's *Rocket* performed so well that they decided it should be an all-locomotive railway from the start.

The Liverpool & Manchester was an instant success with passengers who could travel in greater numbers, faster and cheaper than by stage coach. Almost straight away, work began on other intercity lines, London to Birmingham, Liverpool to Carlisle, London to Bristol and so on. The new lines carried little freight for a year or two until they had built sidings, warehouses and goods yards but then they entered into a sharp price-cutting war with the canals. By 1852 the railways earned more from freight than the canals did.

While this was going on, the Merthyr Tydfil ironmasters were taking the lead in one of the first railways which would carry mostly freight from the start. They met in the Castle Inn, Merthyr Tydfil, on 12 October 1835 to launch the Taff Vale Railway Company, the TVR. Work was finished by April 1841. In September that year the Glamorganshire Canal Company had to cut its freight charges by half to compete.

The TVR was working before the great spurt in railway building throughout Britain, which came with the 'railway mania' of the middle 1840s.

In the 1840s half a million craftsmen and navvies were working on railway building. In 1848, 40% of all home sales of iron went to the railway companies. Orders like source D poured in to the ironworks.

As well as rails there were orders for girders to make bridges and the new stations – two of the kinds of building which began to give Britain the look of an industrialised country. Railways also gave work to a growing number of engineering craftsmen and boiler makers. The larger companies opened their own engineering works to build locomotives, waggons and carriages. For a few years British engineers and ironworks had a world lead in railway products. They supplied the companies which were building the first railways in many parts of the world including Germany and Russia and later India as well as South America and China.

C

Increasing length of railway, 1831–61.

Year	Number of miles in use	Year	Number of miles in use
1831	140	1847	3,945
1835	338	1848	5,127
1840	1,498	1849	6,231
1845	2,441	1850	6,621
1846	3,036	1851	6,877

D

Iron masters to be contracted for the supplying of 6,000 tons of wrought iron rails and a suitable quantity of cast-iron chairs. The rails are to be 15 feet in length, weighing 50 lbs to the yard... the chairs to weigh about 20 lb each the be fitted to these rails and to be cast from the best No 1 quality iron that will file and chip easily. 1,000 tons of the above to be delivered every two months.

London and Southampton Railway Board Minutes, 29 October 1834

3. Roughly how many blast furnaces would be needed to supply 1,000 tons of iron in two months? (See Unit 3E).

E

J.C. Bourne's *The goods shed at Bristol*, painted in 1846. New products and easier freight – the two sides of railways' importance to industry.

4. List the ways in which this scene is evidence for the statement that railways speeded the industrialisation of Britain.
5. How does the picture support the statement that horse-drawn road traffic grew in the mid-nineteenth century?
6. Which two forms of day- and night-lighting were used?
7. Find out how the track of the Great Western Line would be different from that in a station in Birmingham or York.

H SKILLS SECTION

Studying a picture source

In Unit 2F you were asked to show how your knowledge of the background made it easier to understand an eighteenth-century writer. The same skills are needed for studying pictures from past times. Usually they look simple to understand but they can often tell you a lot about historical developments as well as portraying the scene the artists or photographer had in mind. This is a mid-nineteenth-century picture of rope-making.

1. Describe what you can learn from the picture about how ropes were made.
2. What does it tell you about different jobs for men, women and boys.
3. How could you use the picture to point to developments in the iron and engineering industries?
4. Suggest why rope-making would be an important industry by the middle of the nineteenth century.

Knowledge and understanding

For each of the following, explain a) what the job was, b) who usually did it and c) what the job tells you about the industry where it was done.

Piecer
Scavenger
Hewer
Drawer
Puddler

For each of the following explain a) what the term means and b) why it was important to industrial change.

Rotary power
High-pressure
Self-acting
Reverberatory
Air splitting
Locomotive

Look at the pictures in Part Three, apart from 3B. Imagine they were slides which you were using to give a short talk on 'the importance of coal and iron to industry 1780–1850'. Make a brief note to show what you would say about each picture.

About a hundred years ago, a historian first gave the name 'industrial revolution' to the changes you have been studying in Part 3. Explain why you think this phrase is a) accurate, b) misleading.

Before you read on:

The story of the industrial revolution has been taken up to around 1850 but only for the major industries. As you will read in Part 4, industrialisation in the mid-nineteenth century involved far more people than the workers in textiles, iron, coal and machine engineering. There were even large numbers who worked very much as their ancestors had done in 1700.

4

AROUND 1850: THE BRITISH BEE HIVE

    A   Varieties of industrial work
    B   Handworkers and outworkers
    C   Industrialisation and social change
    D   The triumph of free trade
    E   Skills section: summarising 150 years

The British Bee Hive

a) What do you think the artist, George Cruikshank, meant to suggest by calling this the British Bee Hive?
b) Which important groups of workers has he missed out? Can you suggest why?
c) How important does Cruikshank suggest that political freedoms were to the rest of the bee hive?
d) What does he suggest were the two main foundations of British prosperity?

39

A VARIETIES OF WORK

George Cruikshank first designed the British Bee Hive in 1840 and updated it in 1867 so it tells us a lot about how the British saw themselves a few years each side of 1850. They lived in the most industrialised country in the world, and the wealthiest. The average income per head was around £32 compared with about £21 in France and about £13 in Germany. Yet Cruikshank did not sketch any of the industries which have separate units in this book: textiles, iron, mining and railways. That may have been because he was a Londoner and London had few factories and no coal-mines. But it also helps to remind us that the new industries gave work to only about 2 million of the 9½ million people who had jobs at the time of the 1851 census. The others worked in a great variety of trades.

Workshop and small factories

In the 1820s, pens with steel nibs began to replace quills. When the *Illustrated London News* sent its reporter and artist to Birmingham in 1851 there were seventeen pen factories in the town employing about 1,700 people. Only two hundred or so were men. The rest were women working in one of half a dozen rooms where pen nibs were stamped out, pierced, bent, ground and smoothed and finally slit.

There were hundreds of other factories and workshops where unskilled or semi-skilled workers, mostly women, used small machinery to make needles, screws, knives or metal files, buttons and countless other objects. In the pottery industry you would find a room where women fixed handles onto cups, and another where they painted the rims of plates while a smaller number of men worked at the steam-powered machinery which ground the flints and mixed the clay or cared for the furnaces where the pottery was fired.

The machines used in trades such as pen making were

A

1. How would you describe the division between women's and men's work?
2. What industry lay behind the equipment the women are using?
3. Many of these women's mothers might have worked in the metal trades at home or in the first small workshops? What grounds might they have had for a) envying or b) feeling sorry for their daughters?
4. What skills would the editor of the *Illustrated London News* look for in the artists he sent out with reporters?

A1 Men rolling steel.

A2 Women in a slitting room. Both these pictures appeared in the *Illustrated London News*.

possible only because of advances in machine-tool making. A man fitting up the simple machinery in a windmill did not need to work to fine accuracy. If cogs or joints did not fit, the matter was soon solved with a trimming knife or a smart blow with a hammer. Cast-iron parts will only fit and work together if they are accurate to a fraction of a millimetre and if all the screws and bolts have exactly the same thread.

Machine-tool making as a speciality began with the workshop opened by Henry Maudslay in London. He invented lathes for cutting screws, a plane for cutting metal so smooth that two pieces would slide against each other, and a micrometer which could measure down to ten-thousandth of an inch. Many of the leading engineers of the mid-nineteenth century, including James Nasmyth (Unit 3E), were apprenticed to Maudslay. Afterwards all of them moved from London to the industrial north and midlands where they set up their own businesses to make machinery like those in the illustrations. The most important of all was James Whitword who improved on Maudslay's micrometer so that it could measure down to a hundred-thousandth of an inch and who laid down the standard sizes for screw threads that were used until very recently.

The heavy labouring trades

The idea of using the gas from burning coal for lighting was first tried out by William Murdoch, Boulton & Watt's foreman. The partners were so impressed that they put gas lighting into the Soho Manufactory in 1798. It was first used to light a London street in 1805 and street, factory and house lighting spread widely in the 1810s. Widespread use meant that the many gas companies opened works where coal was shovelled into closed furnaces, or retorts, where it was turned into coke, giving off gas which was piped to a gas holder. The coke was pulled out of the retorts while red hot, cooled with water and later sold to ironworks.

There were many other jobs which needed great strength and led to ill-health and many early deaths. Mining was one (Unit 3F), railway building was another. An average day's work for an ordinary navvy was to lift twenty tonnes of 'muck', (his name for earth and rocks) into waggons. The more specialised tunnel workers and bridge builders were so often killed by rockfalls, explosions or falls, that usually no-one bothered to hold an inquest into their death. The growing chemical trade led to many unhealthy jobs. Men shovelled salt cake (made from salt water and sulphuric acid) into furnaces along with coal and lime to make the thousands of tonnes of soda used each year to make bleaching powders. They were easily recognised by their mouths because hydrochloric acid fumes rotted teeth.

Women had their share of the heavy trades. They often worked at the top of mines, breaking ore into smaller lumps to be smelted, or grading and shifting the coal brought up from pits. While men worked in the fierce heat of Merthyr Tydfil ironworks, women made the firebricks used to line the furnaces (see C).

B

A French woman visited the retort room of the Gas Light and Coke Company in the 1830s.

> There were about twenty men...Those who were not doing anything stood motionless, their eyes fixed on the ground, they had not the energy even to wipe off the perspiration streaming from every pore...The foreman told me that stokers were selected from among the strongest, but that nevertheless they all became consumptive after seven or eight years of toil and died of pulmonary consumption...
>
> I asked the foreman where the men, drenched in perspiration, were going to rest themselves.
>
> 'They will throw themselves down on a bed which is under that shed', he said coldly, 'and after a couple of hours they will begin to stoke again.'
>
> The shed, exposed to every wind...is freezing cold...I saw the stokers stretched out on the mattress, which was as hard as a rock. Their only covering was an extremely dirty coat...'That is how' the foreman said, 'the men become consumptive, by going from hot to cold.'

Flora Tristan, *London Journal, a Survey of London Life in the 1830s*

5. What is the modern term for consumption? Would the temperature changes be the only cause?
6. The fathers of many people who did jobs such as this often were immigrants into towns from the countryside. Would they have any reasons to a) envy and b) pity their sons?

C

Underneath the floor are flues for the...heated air, to dry and prepare the bricks for the kilns...

The clay is ground in mills by steam power; and the women then saturate it with cold water... They next temper it with their bare feet, moving rapidly about, with the clay and water reaching to the calf of the leg. This operation completed, they grasp with both arms a lump of clay weighing about 35 pounds, and...carry this load to the moulding table, where other girls, with a plentiful use of cold water, mould it into bricks. They have to feed and attend to the furnaces...in the open air...alternating between the heat of the drying room and the cold winds outside.

Morning Chronicle, 21 March 1850

7. How many bags of sugar would you need to weigh thirty-five pounds?
8. What health hazards would there be in this work?
9. Suggest two reasons why this work was done by women.
10. Would you expect to find men or women in the clay-grinding mills? Why?

B HANDWORKERS AND OUTWORKERS

A

A family of silk weavers in Spitalfields, east London, 1861.

1. List the ways in which this scene could be typical of manufacturing 150 years before.

B

A knitter's account of his fellow workers in 1845.

> They stand at the ends of the streets; and some will go and beg for weeks rather than take the work at a reduced price...others will take to poaching ...other men, who have been determined not to endure the suffering, have gone in sneakish manner across the fields to Leicester with a bag over their shoulder to fetch a bit of work, and do it and under price, without saying anything about it.

Royal Commission on the Condition of the Framework Knitters, 1845

2. Why should a man need to collect work 'in a sneakish manner'?

C

There were few factories in hosiery towns such as Nottingham and Leicester but a common sight was a terrace of framework knitters cottages. These were built in about 1800.

3. How can you tell that these were knitters' homes?
4. What do they suggest about the knitters who lived in them compared with those in Source B?
5. When do you think the photograph was taken?

There were at least as many handworkers in 1851 as in the early eighteenth century. Since then the total population had risen from 5 to 21 million, quite enough to supply all the workers in the modern industries of the time as well as the huge numbers still in the old hand trades. There were also far more people to buy hand-made goods especially now that most working families no longer made their own clothes, candles and furniture. But extra work did not mean good times for handworkers. Some products, such as silk cloth, went mostly to the rich but even then wages were low and hours were long – as the picture suggests. Other handworkers suffered from the fact that the merchants kept wages for home working low so they could sell at low prices to the new working class.

Handwork for men and families

In the stocking trade of the east midlands all the knitting was done on hand frames until the first steam factory was opened in Nottingham in 1851. A few workers probably earned good money. They were the ones who made the finer hose in the attics of their homes near the merchants' warehouses in the larger towns. But for twenty or thirty miles around, there were villages where handloom knitting was the only work open to men. There were so many that masters were able to force the piece rates down so that by 1842 they were hardly more than half the amount paid in 1814.

Silk weaving and framework knitting were family trades where the man was the main operative helped by his wife and children. This was also true of the 250,000 people making boots and shoes in 1851. The process began in workshops where men cut out the shapes for the bottoms and uppers. These were sent to the homes of outworkers. Here, children waxed the thread and punched holes in the leather, women stitched the parts of the upper together and men fitted the upper to a sole and added the heel.

Handwork for women and girls

In the more agricultural counties there was still a lot of handwork done mostly by women and children. One example was glove-making.

D

A glove manufacturer explains his business.

> The material is sent in the piece from London to the agent in some central place in Somersetshire, Devonshire, Worcestershire...On his premises a few men are employed to cut out, and then the various parts of the glove are given out to be sewn together. The people who do that are the wives and daughters of agricultural labourers scattered through the neighbouring country...If they live near they bring in their work as it is finished; if far off someone goes round once a fortnight and collects all that is ready...
>
> *Report of the Royal Commission on Children's Employment*, 1864

6. List the ways in which this was similar to the descriptions of domestic work in Units 1A and 1B.

Women and children in the countries around London worked at lace-making and plaiting straw which was made into hats and bonnets. Many of the children did their daily stint in a lace or a plaiting 'school'. Very few made any pretence of teaching except sometimes a little reading. Most were single rooms where one woman kept children at work until they had finished the lace or straw that their parents had given them in the morning.

E

A twelve-year-old boy describes his plaiting school, 1843:

> Come to work pretty nigh always at nine in the morning, leave off at six in the evening if we've done our set, if we aren't we sit till we've done...earn about 1s 6d a week, from which I pay 3d schooling. Mrs Demock teaches some on 'em to read, not me. Father is out of work, mother works at the bonnet; one brother works at the willow here also;...mistress whacks with a stick when they sit idle.
>
> *Royal Commission on Children's Employment*, 1843

7. What was the real purpose of this school?

Labourers and casual workers

A tremendous number of jobs were done by sheer physical labour because a mechanical way of making things or shifting goods had not been developed. Most warehouses had a simple hoist crane jutting out from an upper room but goods still had to be back-packed.

F

Liverpool dockers in 1835.

> These men (chiefly Irishmen) received the full sacks as they were lowered by the crane...and carried them across the road. They pursued their heavy task during the working hours of a summer's day at...a trot of at least five miles an hour, the distance from the vessel to the storehouse being a full fifty yards...a good labourer...made 750 trips from the warehouse to the vessel, carrying for half the distance a full sack of oats on his shoulder, thus performing a distance of...43 miles nearly.
>
> Sir G. Head, *A Home Tour Through the Manufacturing Districts of England in the Summer of 1835*, 1836

8. How does this work compare with the longest walk and the heaviest load you have carried?

The streets of towns teemed with people doing poorly-paid jobs, such as earning tips by sweeping a road-crossing clean of mud and horse dung or selling every kind of item. In 1852 the reporter, Henry Mayhew, published accounts of interviews with these workers:

G

The water-cress seller.

> The poor child, although the weather was severe, was dressed in a thin cotton gown, with a threadbare shawl wrapped around her shoulders. She wore no covering to her head and her long rusty hair stood out in all directions. When she walked she shuffled along for fear that the large carpet slippers that served her for shoes would slip off...
> "I go about the streets with water-creases, crying 'Four bunches a penny, water-creases.' I am just eight years old..."

The crossing sweeper.

> Those who think that sweepin' a crossing is idle work, make a great mistake. In wet weather, the traffic makes it get sloppy as soon as it's cleaned. Cabs and 'buses, and carriages continually going over the crossing must scatter mud on it and you must look precious sharp to keep it clean...I gives threepence for my brooms. I wears out three in a week in the wet weather.
>
> H. Mayhew, *London Life and the London Poor*, 1852

9. Do these two jobs have anything in common?

C INDUSTRIALISATION AND SOCIAL CHANGE

The 1851 Census showed that one in four people lived in a town of over 100,000 and one in every 2½ in a town of over 20,000. In 1700 there were only three towns of that size. The change had come about in two ways.

Migration

Migration was the first cause of the growth of towns. In 1851 only a quarter of the people in Manchester and Bradford had been born there. Many of the others had come as young adults.

A

A1 Home life in the villages.

Home has no attraction for the young labourer. When he goes there, tired and chilly, he is in the way amidst domestic discomforts; the cottage is small, the children are troublesome, the fire is diminished, the solitary candle is lighted late and extinguished early...

Agricultural Review, 1853

A2 Rural housing in Leicestershire.

Look at the hovels, made of mud and straw; bits of glass, or of old cast-off windows, without frames or hinges frequently, but merely stuck in the mud wall. Enter them, and look at the bits of chairs or stool; the wretched boards tacked together to serve as a table; the floor of pebble, broken brick or of the bare ground; look at the thing called a bed; and survey the rags on the back of the wretched inhabitants.

William Cobbett, *Rural Rides*, Vol 2, 1830

1. Use these extracts to suggest why village people were prepared to move to over-crowded towns.
2. What other explanations might there be?

When English people left such conditions they generally moved only a few miles to a nearby town. Migrants from the Scottish Highlands and Ireland came much further to escape poverty and even famine. An important result of all the migration was that the most densely populated areas were in the north of England and central Scotland. In the eighteenth century they had been in the south of England.

Birth and death

The second cause of growing towns was 'natural increase', the difference between the numbers born and dying. If a young man and woman moved to a town and married or lived together, there would likely be four or five extra people very soon, once they started a family. One of the results was that Britain was a country of young people. In 1851, 76% were under forty and 45% under nineteen. When it came to deaths, the industrial towns showed an alarming trend as source B shows.

Information such as this could be added to the piles of facts from many private enquiries into just what living conditions were like (see C).

C Three standards of living

C1 In the skilled workers' cottages.

The cottages are built of stone, and contain from four to six rooms each; back-premises with suitable conveniences are attached to them all...I visited the interior of nearly every cottage and found...there were generally a mahogany table and a chest of drawers. Daughters from most of the houses, but wives, as far as I could learn, from none, worked in the factory. Many of the women ...exhibited the Sunday wardrobes of their husbands, the stock of neatly folded shirts etc.

William Cooke Taylor, *Notes of a Tour*, 1842

B

Comparative death rates from the *Census Report* of 1841.

3. Of every 100,000 born how many were alive at these ages in a) Liverpool and b) Surrey: 5 years; 15; 30; 50?
4. List the possible reasons you can think of for the difference.

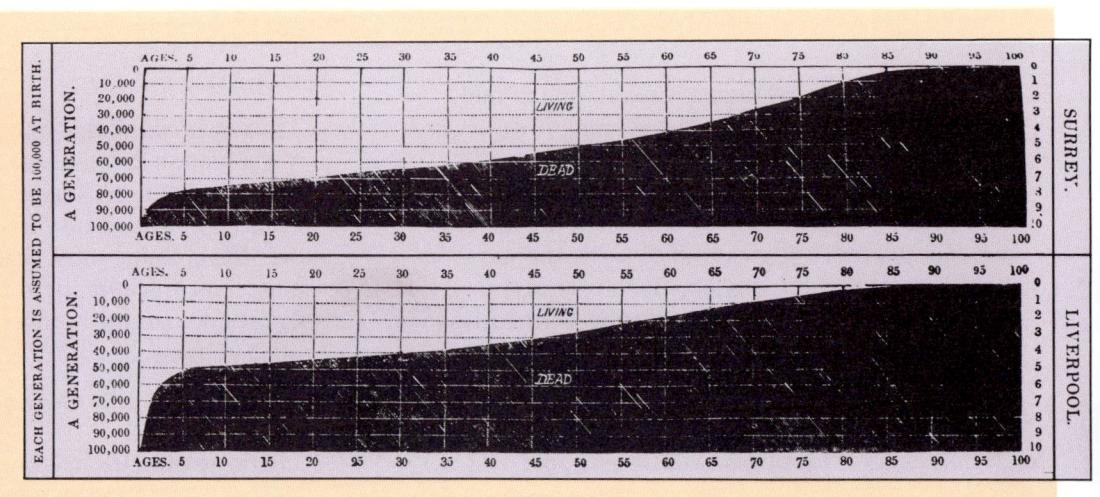

C Three standards of living

C2 In factory hands' back-to-backs.

They are built back-to-back, with no possibility of good ventilation, and contain a cellar for coals and food, the coal department being frequently tenanted with fowls, pigeons or rabbits...a room from 9 to 14 feet by from 10 to 12 or 14 feet, to do all the cooking, washing...and another of the same size to sleep in. Think for a moment what must be the inconvenience, the danger both in a moral and physical sense, when parents and children, young men and women, married and single, are crowded together in this way, with three beds in a room, and barely a couple of yards in the middle.

Annual Report of the Domestic Mission Society, Leeds, 1854

C3 Cellar dwellings.

I have been in one of these damp cellars, without the slightest drainage, every drop of wet and every morsel of dirt and filth having to be carried up into the street; two corded frames for beds, overlaid with sacks for five persons; scarcely anything in the room else to sit on but a stool or a few bricks; the floor, in many places, absolutely wet; a pig in the corner also.

Robert Baker, *Report on the Condition of the Residences of the Labouring Classes in the town of Leeds*, 1842

5. What is meant in C1 by 'back-premises with suitable conveniences'?
6. Explain which details in these sources could account for the facts shown in the chart comparing Liverpool and Surrey.

D

Average earnings in a Leeds spinning mill, 1840.

| Men | | Women and Girls | | Children (under 14) | |
No. employed	Average weekly wage	No. employed	Average weekly wage	No. employed	Average weekly wage
135	21s 8d	478	5s 11½d	409	2s 5d

7. Imagine a family with one man, his wife, a teenage daughter and a ten-year-old. What would their family earnings amount to?

The factor which led to such differences in living-conditions was the family's earning power. The best-paid were the skilled workers or artisans. There would be no women amongst them. In the eighteenth century most would have worked in crafts such as carpentry and masonry. By 1851 their numbers had been swelled by mechanical engineers, locomotive drivers, iron puddlers, and first-grade mule spinners. They earned up to forty shillings a week and could afford homes like those in Source C1. Most paid a weekly subscription to a friendly society which would help them in times of sickness. Many paid around nine pence a week to send their sons to a private writing school where they could learn reading, writing and arithmetic.

The middle ranks of the working classes were filled with semi-skilled people who were 'operatives' in mills, iron works, and workshops as well as workers such as miners. Men, women and children worked in different parts of factories, but the total family earnings were still what mattered – as they had in their grandparents' day.

A hard-working family with children at the right age might rent a house like that in C1, especially if they had a lodger which was common because of the large numbers of new immigrants to towns. But there was unemployment when trade was bad, and no cover for sickness or old age. So they usually ended up in a back-to-back house. The better ones were two-up, two-down, but many had only one room on each floor like the house in C2. An operative's children usually had no more than two or three year's schooling, often part-time, in a factory school or a 'monitorial school'.

The poorest ranks of the working classes held those who earned no more than 10s. Many were handworkers like the stocking knitters whose best wages in the 1840s were 7s a week. Others were labourers in gas-works or on building sites or people with casual earnings such as street-sellers and crossing sweepers. Few children went to any school, and housing was squalid. Single people often lived, a dozen or more to a room, in a common lodging house. Families rented a room in a decaying large house or lived in a cellar like that in C3.

E

Manchester mill operatives.

8. The artist included a first-grade mule spinner and the knocker-up who woke families in time to start their day's work. Can you identify them?
9. In which way does the picture support Source C?
10. What do you notice about the position of the mills and houses?

D THE TRIUMPH OF FREE TRADE

The world's first trade fair

There had been several trade exhibitions in France and England for national products only. It was the Queen's husband, Prince Albert, who suggested that Britain should hold 'an Exhibition of the Works of Industry of all Nations'. In a private note he wrote that 'particular advantage to British industry might be derived from placing it in fair competition with that of other Nations.'

Opening day was 1 May 1851, following nine months of furious activity to build the Crystal Palace (as the exhibition halls were named by Punch magazine). 4,500 tons of iron girders and gutters were hauled into place by horses straining on the ropes which pulled them to the top of huge cranes. Nearly 300,000 pieces of sheet glass (a new invention of 1832) were fitted by men moving forward in trolleys which ran in the gutters.

Just over half the 14,000 exhibitors were British and the Great Exhibition seemed to prove that Britain deserved the title 'workshop of the world'. On show were dozens of the machines which turned out the textiles and iron goods she sold in every continent, the locomotives, carriages and bridge sections that were taking the railway age to Europe, India, the West Indies and America, and, of course, the machine-tools which made all this possible.

A

British machinery in the Crystal Palace.

1. What impression does this give of Britain's progress as an industrialised country?
2. Why was 'Crystal Palace' a good name for the building?

Many people noted the smaller signs of Britain's prosperity, especially on the cheap days when the railway excursions flooded the halls with working people from all over the country. A few farm labourers still came in smocks but the townspeople came in fustian jackets and trousers, cotton shirts and dresses. They drank soda-water or ginger ale (no alcohol) out of one of the million standardised bottles supplied by Messers Schweppes. They went home to sleep in a mass-produced iron bedstead and perhaps dream of the day when they could afford a brass one or a carpet which had become standard in middle-class homes. Next evening they might light the oil-lamp or just possibly the gas-light with a match (Dad's old tinder box was now an ornament) and sit down to write a letter with a steel-nibbed pen, place it in the latest invention – 'little sacks of paper called envelopes' – and send it anywhere for 1d.

B

A mill-owner wrote in his diary in 1853:

> ...I have never seen clearer evidence of general well-being. Our country is, no doubt, in a most happy and prosperous state. Free trade, peace and freedom. O, happy England.
>
> A. Watkin, *Extracts from his journal, 1814–56*, ed. A.E. Watkin, Unwin, 1920

3. From Units 4A–4C, how far would you agree that England was happy and prosperous.
4. Look back at the beehive (page 39). In which ways did the mill-owner and the artist agree?

Exports and imports

C

Britain's share of world industrial production.

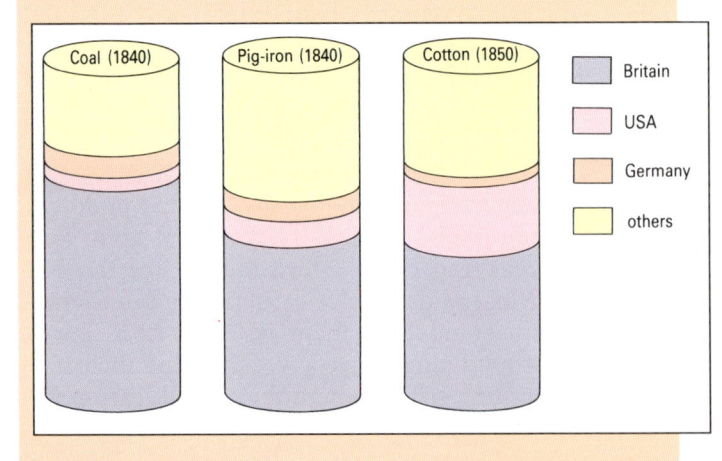

[Bar chart showing Coal (1840), Pig-iron (1840), Cotton (1850) with shares for Britain, USA, Germany, others]

5. What do these show about the importance of the industries in Part 3?

The price of textiles fell with the coming of large-scale factory production. At home, the money needed to buy a yard of muslin in 1790 could buy sixty-seven yards in 1830. Overseas, British cloth was so cheap that it could be sold in countries which had their own strong hand-working industries. In the early eighteenth century, India had exported cottons, muslins and calicos to Britain. By 1850 she had become the largest single market for British cotton cloth, buying more than the whole of Europe and the Middle East put together. Another major new market for textiles was the countries of Latin America which bought cotton and worsted cloths. In 1784, when they were still Spanish colonies, Britain had exported £7,000 worth of goods there. By 1854 the figure had risen to £9 million.

European traders came to Britain to buy semi-manufactured goods which could be used by their own new industries. British cotton and wool spinners sent huge quantities of yarn while iron-masters sold them pig-iron, wrought-iron bars, plates and girders. Some Europeans bought British machinery for their textile factories and in the 1840s they began to buy locomotives and other railway equipment. Europe also bought British coal. Exports, mostly from Welsh pits, rose from 0.2 million tons to 3.2 million between 1800 and 1850.

Raw materials are vital to an industrial nation. The list was headed by cotton which poured in through Liverpool from the southern states of the USA. Timber had second place because of its importance for building, pit props, railway sleepers and so on. The third was wool. The Yorkshire worsted industry imported long fibred wool from Germany which came off the backs of Merino sheep which were first bred in Spain. Merinos were taken to Australia and by the 1840s imports from this fast-growing British colony began to overtake those from Germany. Britain also grew fast in population and had to import food or starve. The leading food import was grain from Russia and the Baltic countries.

Protection or free trade

By the 1820s many industrialists looked on protectionism as a barrier not as an encouragement to trade. They thought it more important to get supplies of raw material than to bother about whose ship they were carried in or whose colony they came from. They believed that allowing machinery to be exported or skilled mechanics to emigrate would do more good than harm by helping to create markets for yarn, iron and machines.

Many government ministers and officials in the Board of Trade were in favour of freeing trade. Step by step they relaxed the rules. Ministers such as William Huskisson in the 1820s and Robert Peel in the 1840s cut duties on imports. From the 1820s it was no longer illegal for machinery or skilled workers to go abroad. Yet there was a political obstacle to completely free trade. It came from the landowners and large farmers, especially those who grew wheat. In 1815 Parliament had passed the Corn Laws which put a high duty on imported corn so that the price of home-grown wheat would not slump because of competition from imports.

In 1838 a group of Lancashire manufacturers and politicians set up the anti-Corn Law League. The strongest argument in their pamphlets and public meetings was that the end of the Corn Laws would mean cheaper bread for everyone. Their newspaper was called *The anti-Bread Tax Circular*. In this way they hoped to win the support of working people, but the workers' leaders usually replied that cheaper bread would lead to lower wages. In any case, the real aim of the anti-Corn Law League was to end import duties on foreign goods so that Britain could, in turn, persuade other countries to cut their protection duties and let in British manufactures at a lower price.

The Corn Laws were repealed after the government had to buy large amounts of cheap foreign corn to help the victims of the famine which was sweeping Ireland (then part of the United Kingdom). It was a nonsense to have one part of the country eating the cheapest possible grain and the rest having to pay prices which depended on the Corn Laws. Parliament repealed them and then set about abolishing all the other examples of restriction on trade. Two hundred years of protection came to an end when the Navigation Laws were repealed in 1849. Free trade lasted until the early twentieth century when other countries' industries were to rival Britain's and manufacturers complained that low foreign prices were putting them and their workpeople out of business.

D

Britain's trading partners, 1854–6.

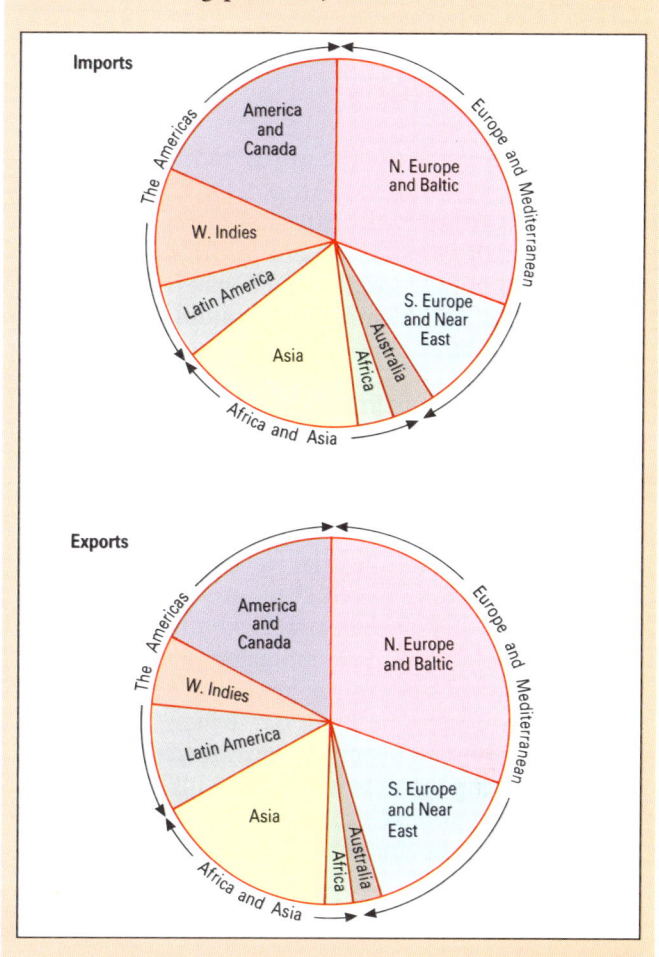

6. Compare these with the charts on page 20. Which are the most important changes in exports and imports. How do you account for them?

E SKILLS SECTION

Interpretations

The first person to use the words 'industrial revolution' was Professor Arnold Toynbee in lectures he gave to Oxford University students in 1880–1. Since then almost all historians in Britain have agreed that a 'revolution' took place somewhere between the middle of the eighteenth and the middle of the nineteenth centuries.

Two historians explain why they believe that the industrial changes add up to a revolution.

A

> Essentially the Industrial Revolution created the sort of society with which we are familiar... The Industrial Revolution was the great watershed in recent history, dividing what we know as modern England from all previous types of society... It offered to men, for the first time in human history, the way towards controlling their environment... The possibility of material abundance for all was no longer an idle dream.
>
> J.F.C. Harrison, *The Common People*, Fontana, 1984

1. Each sentence gives one main reason for saying that the industrial revolution was a great event. How would you summarise them?
2. Explain, with examples, what J.F.C. Harrison means by 'controlling their environment' and 'the possibility of material abundance for all'.

B

> Industrialisation in turn is at the heart of a larger, more complex process often designated as modernisation... Modernisation comprises such developments as urbanisation... a sharp reduction in both death rates and birth rates from traditional levels,... the establishment of a... fairly centralised bureaucratic government; the creation of an educational system capable of training and socialising the children of the society... and, of course, the acquisition of the ability and the means to use an up-to-date technology.
>
> D.S. Landes, *The Unbound Prometheus*, CUP, 1969

3. Compare this list of aspects of modernisation with the syllabus in British history that you are studying. How far does it cover the same topics? Are there any important differences?

Historians agree that a revolution took place but often argue about when it began. Arnold Toynbee dated it from 1760 but the American historian, J.U. Nef said it began much earlier and the British historian T.S. Ashton gave his reasons for putting the beginning in the 1780s.

C

C1

> The rise of industrialism in Britain can be more properly regarded as a long process stretching back to the middle of the sixteenth century and coming down to the final triumph of the industrial state towards the end of the nineteenth.
>
> J.U. Nef, in *Economic History Review*, 1934

C2

> After 1782 almost every available statistical series of industrial output reveals a sharp upward turn. More than half the growth in the shipments of coal and the mining of copper, more than three-quarters of the increase of broad cloths, four-fifths of that of printed cloth and nine-tenths of the exports of cotton goods were concentrated in the last eighteen years of the century.
>
> T.S. Ashton, *The Eighteenth Century*, Methuen, 1955

5. Choose evidence and sources from this book to support the view that the industrial revolution can be traced back to a) 1700–50, b) the 1760s, c) the 1780s.

D

The historian Eric Hobsbawm wrote in *The Age of Revolution* that 'Words are witnesses which speak louder than documents.' He gave a list of new words which appeared between the 1780s and the 1850s. They included:

industry	crisis (economic)
capitalism	railway
sociology	working class
pauperism	factory
middle class	statistics
industrialist	strike
socialism	engineer

6. Which of these is no longer in everyday use? Why has it fallen out of the language?